NEW TESTAMENT FAITH FOR TODAY

NEW TESTAMENT
FAITH
FOR TODAY

by

AMOS N. WILDER

SCM PRESS LTD
56 BLOOMSBURY STREET
LONDON

First British edition 1956

*Printed in Great Britain by
Billing and Sons Ltd., Guildford and London*

For C. D. W. *and* A. T. W.

. . . Therefore plunge anchors in the heart of love
Now in the calm before the risen sea
Scatter the barques and veil the heavens above;
And *lay great bases for eternity:*
Now in the fragile hour's brief endeavor
Knit a society that naught can sever.

contents

7

fOREWORÒ

The interpreter of the Bible today must reconcile two somewhat different tasks. He must make clear how alien its assumptions and conceptions are from those of today, thus
safeguarding major insights, however much of scandal they
may involve for modern thinking. Next, from this point of
vantage or disadvantage he must seek to convey this body of
thought and faith in the most persuasive way possible to a
different age. For such persuasion he relies on the unchanging
needs of men, but also upon those shocks in contemporary
experience which unmask current sophistries and dispose men
to a profounder hearing. The community of faith rests from
of old upon momentous disclosures as to our life, its origins
and goal. Modern experience, modern findings in the human
sciences, and more significantly still, modern extremity, bring
hosts of men within hailing distance of this heritage, even as
they quicken the grasp upon it of those who count themselves
among the believers. It is hoped that these chapters may remove some of the misconceptions which hinder this repossess-
sion of the living tradition.

Four of the following chapters rest upon lectures given in
1948 at the School of Religion of Butler University.[1] They
have been much expanded and rewritten. I still bear in mind

[1] Published in *The Shane Quarterly*, vol. 9, no. 2 (April, 1948) with
the title, "New Testament Faith and Its Relevance Today." Copyright,
1948, by the School of Religion, Butler University. Part of Chapter IV,
"The Message of Paul," as it appeared in *The Shane Quarterly*, was
quoted by Thomas S. Kepler in his *Contemporary Thinking about Paul*
(Abingdon Press, 1950).

the courtesies at that time of Dean Orman L. Shelton and the Faculty of the School.

Appreciation is expressed to the Conference on Science, Philosophy and Religion for permission to reprint Chapter II, "The Language of Faith," which originally appeared under the title "Myth and Symbol in the New Testament" in *Symbols and Values: An Initial Study,* edited by Lyman Bryson, Louis Finkelstein, R. M. MacIver and Richard McKeon (Harper, 1954).

Quotations from the Bible are in almost all cases from the Revised Standard Bible. and acknowledgment is here gratefully made to the International Council of Religious Education.

Amos N. Wilder

Cambridge, Massachusetts
January, 1955

1

commenoing the gospel
in our time

Each one heard them speaking in his own language.
Acts 2:6

All men presumably live by some kind or portion of faith,
articulate or inarticulate. It is sometimes said that when all
faith goes, suicide is the inevitable alternative. This has recently been denied by a contemporary school of thoroughgoing
atheists who find elation and an incentive to live in the sheer
absurdity of the world and in man's freedom to make his own
future. But faith is hidden under this revulsion against inherited stereotypes of belief. Men can live by false faiths, for a
time, and men can meanly exist on the basis of a meager faith.
But when faith is impoverished it leads to apathy and sloth
which are a form of suicide, or it turns to fear and that also
takes suicidal forms, social and individual. Faith and life come
together and go together. Faith is the breath of life.

Christianity came into the world as a faith, in the sense both
of a dynamic impulse and a world-shaping and life-shaping
vision. This means an enormous confidence and security in
existence and an assured understanding of the way and goal of
the world. This faith is a difficult one to accept not only because of the evidence that seems to contradict it but also
because the direction and meaning of life which it affirms are
ruthlessly exclusive of other directions and meanings. But for
those who apprehend it or who are apprehended by it, floods

of light are shed upon the ultimate enigmas, the Sphinx receives its answer, the queries and expostulations of Job are quieted, and evil is not simply endured but overcome and transmuted. The Christian does not claim to be always illumined or always faithful, but he knows that he is never abandoned, and he is sure that the world never falls out of the hands of God. Such security rightly understood does not make for irresponsibility but the converse. It is true that Christians belie their profession, betray their calling and bring the faith into disrepute. This can only mean their forfeiture of the life of faith in greater or lesser degree and the endangering of their own souls. But it should not obscure the true character of the Christian way.

This faith as a particular vision of man and the world, as a confident affirmation of the direction and meaning of life, necessarily involves doctrine. From the writings of the New Testament on through the classic formulations of the church and right down to the testimony of preacher and theologian today, Christians have insisted on their own reading of the world and their knowledge of its character. Doctrine in this sense cannot be surrendered despite our modern recognition of the changing character of the words we use. There is a tendency today, especially in some forms of liberal Judaism, to waive the truth aspect of religion and to exalt its inherited ceremonies and ethics as community-preserving and community-shaping forces. Are not the doctrinal aspects of religion divisive? And is it not true that believers always sooner or later freeze their doctrines into shibboleths which foreclose the freedom of both mind and spirit? Yet neither the faith of Christians nor the faith of Israel can forego doctrine. It is in our testimony as to the character of the world that ethics and community rite are grounded. It is, indeed, disastrous if we allow the tenets of our faith to become stereotypes. Just as our attitude to the symbols of ritual can become "a sort of sensuous idolatry" (Santayana), so our attitude to creed and doctrine can become a sort of conceptual idolatry. But belief can be true without being tyrannical, and the truth in question is the perennial glory of Christianity through all its vicissitudes.

Faith, then, always involves doctrine, but it is always richer than any particular formulation. The realities in question awaken in us such a wealth of profound apprehensions that the most adequate statement of faith will always have a pictorial and imaginative character. It is with this kind of language that faith speaks. To grasp the full witness of the New Testament we must give heed to what is implicit as well as explicit, to the assumptions as well as the doctrines, and to the symbolic and figurative elements as well as to what appears to be more directly stated. It is important to stress this because our contemporaries are inclined to countenance only "clear ideas" and to undervalue imaginative presentation. Thus they miss aspects of insight and wisdom which reason, even generously defined, does not take into account.

I

Our interest in the question of relevance requires that we understand the attitudes of modern men to the Bible and to biblical faith. The contemporary dilemma with regard to the Christian religion is a highly complex one. Apologists commonly oversimplify the matter. Much of what they say in condemnation of "secularism" is no doubt true. Modern society has become alienated from its religious traditions in a marked degree. Yet Christian faith takes many forms and hides under many disguises. We should always be more concerned about real idolatry or self-sufficiency wherever found than about secular labels or ecclesiastical statistics.

The fact is that in the conditions of today hosts of men are puzzled and tacit as to their belief, dubious and intermittent as to formal affiliation with the religious institutions, but not fundamentally alienated. We are in an interim period between an old and a new formulation of the Christian religion. The world has moved into a new climate which makes the standing patterns of church, worship and doctrine increasingly unreal and unrelated. The sons and daughters of devout forebears, according as they are exposed to the new influences, are led often by their own integrity to detach themselves from the existing religious forms. It follows that certain of the best elements of society carry on a deeply Christianized way of life at some remove from the main stream of the faith. There have been similar critical periods when a reconception of our religion was demanded by the conditions of a new age or a new region. Such epochs are periods of explorations, uncertainty, schism and heresy. The true solutions often arise in unexpected circles. Adequate repossession of the Christian faith today depends to a peculiar degree upon a new encounter with the Bible. This is not possible unless a significant revision can be effected in many long-standing attitudes to it both inside and outside the churches.

Thus anyone who undertakes today to defend and interpret the Christian faith should have all the acquaintance he can with the alienated masses and their outlook, and with the values, ideals and errors which shape modern attitudes. Some of the errors we face are very deeply rooted. These cannot be overthrown apart from general historical convulsions. "When thy judgments are in the earth, the inhabitants of the world learn righteousness" (Is. 26:9). That is the kind of period in which we are living, and in many quarters we find old resistances breaking down. But the faith still meets invincible ignorance among many groups and elsewhere even malignant antagonists. In certain respects our society today relates itself to the church as the Roman Empire did to the first believers. The climate of modern culture has brought forth not only alienated and secularized strata but also definitely anti-Christian movements. The latter often hold that religion is an escape mechanism or opiate, or at least that it is commonly so perverted. They can crassly explain away even its supreme manifestations by some social or psychological theory. The God-idea and the Christ-concept are explained as naïve projections. Immortality is viewed as a compensatory dream. All such religious beliefs with their institutions and rites are viewed as enervating and stultifying. The plausibility of this opinion is well suggested in a recent novel, in which Julius Caesar, reflecting on the practices of augury and divination of the Romans, makes the following comment:

Most of all, however, these observances attack and undermine the very spirit of life within the minds of men. They afford to our Romans, from the street-sweepers to the consuls, a vague sense of confidence where no confidence is and at the same time a pervasive fear, a fear which neither arouses to action nor calls forth ingenuity, but which paralyzes. They remove from men's shoulders the unremitting obligation to create, moment by moment, their own Rome. They come to us sanctioned by our childhood; they flatter our passivity and console inadequacy . . . what can I do against the apathy that is glad to wrap itself under the cloke of piety . . . ?[1]

[1] Thornton Wilder, *The Ides of March* (London: Longmans, 1948), p. 3.

An analogous suspicion of religion or hostility to it today penetrates into the church itself, and is sufficiently well grounded to confuse the issues seriously. It colors the thinking and paralyzes the adhesion of countless men and women and families who stand on its threshold, neither in nor out of the faith.

Yet, we repeat, we should not exaggerate the extent of de-Christianization in our society. A residual and inarticulate Christian disposition survives in our secularized population like a water table that has receded into the subsoil. It still gives evidence of itself in our institutions and public life. It operates as an unrecognized conscience in the individual and the nation, if only to trouble us. But this kind of latent religion is not vigorous enough to detect and resist the powerful seductions of false faiths and the Pied Pipers of destruction. And apart from the great calamities, there are always with us the victims of our impersonal scheme of life, with its neglect, ravage and heartbreak.

Indeed, the perennial difficulty of being a Christian, whether in conduct or in faith, takes on its special form today. There are many men and women about us, disabused and clairvoyant, for whom the standing axioms and familiar apologetic of the churches have broken down. Like Job they cling to an ultimate blind trust, but they feel that they have been fed on half-truths. Confusions with regard to the Bible accentuate the dilemma. The Bible's realism actually accords with the soberest modern thinking, and its faith actually begins at the point of disenchantment where many live today. But even the New Testament represents such a large question mark for most men that the help it could give is greatly hindered. There results an unnecessary skepticism with regard to the origins of our faith. Men are also more aware of the alienness of the thought world in which the leading figures of the New Testament moved. The main symbols in which the faith is couched are strange. Its outlook appears naïve, its mood otherworldly and its ethics impracticable.

All the great anti-Christian movements of the nineteenth and twentieth centuries involve gross misunderstanding of the Bible and of Christian origins. Marxists could not impose their view of the economic determination of religions so easily if they had a more correct understanding of the rise of Christianity. Nazism was facilitated by the plausibility with which its Aryan theories were forced on the Gospels. Excessive confidence in science or in technology today find easy rootage where multitudes accept views at third hand that the primitive Christian faith was an otherworldly and ascetic form of escapism, and that its ethic was a slave morality. Some of the nobler types of humanism today are blocked from their proper fulfillment by erroneous views of the Bible and of Christ for which both friends and foes of Christianity are responsible.

The case of the great French humanist André Gide is representative here. Bred in a powerful Protestant outlook, and continuing throughout his life to appeal to Christ and the Gospels as he understood them, he nevertheless failed to lay hold of the Christian faith adequately. "The cross triumphed over Christ," he wrote; "it was Christ crucified that continued to be seen, and taught. . . . And thus it was that this religion succeeded in darkening the world." And he could conclude that "any religion, whatever it is, when it wins out and can impose itself, sacrifices man and dissuades him from all progress." But as a recent biographer has shown, this great empiricist appears never to have made a careful study of biblical criticism, or of the best modern understanding of Christian

B

origins.[2] He deals with many central matters in the Gospels but usually on the basis of a private interpretation. It has often been remarked that many intellectuals and scientists who are scrupulous about their learning in other respects rest for a lifetime on the picture of Christianity which they had when they withdrew from the Sunday School in adolescence.

Nevertheless, the movements against faith in our time do render us a service. They are exposing and undermining "the things that can be shaken," so that we can more easily identify the things that cannot be shaken. The edifice of faith in which men live today has parts that are built of wood, hay and stubble, and often we do not or cannot distinguish between them. But the construction is being tested by fire and all that is shoddy or flimsy is being unmasked. As Paul says, "The day will declare it." The lucidity and realism and even the bitterness of modern skepticism make their contribution here. They too help us to find that in our faith which is indestructible.

II

We may apply here a thesis of A. J. Toynbee to support our hope for the renewal of the Christian faith. The breakdown of civilization is recurrently the occasion for the rise of a new religion or the reflowering of an old. As old securities go, men are forced back upon their ultimate resources and the conditions are favorable for a renewed creative vision of life and for new community forms and symbols. When we consider the universal character of the present cultural and social disarray it is not surprising that the rebirth of the Christian

[2] Van Meter Ames, *André Gide* (New York: New Directions, 1947), p. 80.

faith is long delayed and difficult. Its own universal character, however, destines it peculiarly to serve the special task of our age, the building of a world community, a task dramatized by two world wars.

For the catastrophes of our time are best understood as the birth pangs of a new world order. The wars, convulsions and disorders of our century have their antecedents in a long past and are not to be put down chiefly to the evil machinations of dictators and other scapegoats. And we should look not only at the costs of so great a transition, nor think only of what is uprooted and overthrown. We should look forward with eager expectations to the *new* world and in some real sense the *one* world that will emerge from these throes. So doing we may well ask ourselves whether the Christian church with all its sectarian divisions can serve such a future, a future that is now already upon us, and a future that properly requires a church that transcends sect, race and nation. Can a divided church even survive in such a future?

But it is not only with respect to their divisions that the churches belong to the old order. Their very spirit is characterized by the values of an age that has been found wanting. The world that is coming to birth reflects the aspirations of the masses of mankind in East and West for a more abundant life, for social and cultural patterns that transcend the mediocrity, conformity, materialism and caste structures of the past. And we may well ask ourselves again whether the Christian churches, deeply marked by these same patterns of the old order, can fulfill their providential role in such a future or even survive in it.

Only the church as it is called of God, and not the church as it actually is, has the universality and the purity to meet this fateful occasion. The time imposes upon the Christian faith, as upon all our significant traditions, a radical renewal and reconception. Fortunately, this necessity has been anticipated in many ways by the leading of the Spirit. In movements toward Christian unity, in the quickening of theology, in a return to the Bible and in the bright flame of Christian life in many of the younger churches of Africa and the East, the way has been prepared for a new Reformation. But quite outside the churches spiritual movements in the life of the West have augured a deepening of the Christian tradition. For at least a century and a half a series of remarkable rebels, secular prophets and artists have arisen as critics of the churches and their values, critics of both Catholicism and Protestantism, of both orthodoxy and liberalism. During this period the churches have themselves so widely faltered and erred that their own heretics have served the true cause and been justified. We have in mind figures like Blake and Shelley, Emerson and Whitman, Nietzsche and Gide, D. H. Lawrence and W. B. Yeats, to speak only of writers. Men of this kind have stood apart from the philistinism and narrow loyalties of their age, have represented insights neglected in both church and society and have voiced the demands of the modern world for more adequate versions of its religious traditions. For all the error to be associated with the agnostics and iconoclasts of the nineteenth century, they, together with the great scientists and creative thinkers of the age, have administered salutary shocks to Christendom and given a lead to the renewal of the faith in a time like ours of "the shaking of the foundations." The Spirit has been at work here as it has been within the churches themselves preparing the Christian faith for that renewal which alone can serve the crisis of the age even as it draws strength from it.

It is, however, of the utmost importance that the true continuity of the Christian faith be maintained, and that an august and vivid sense of the original movement be available for this task of reconstruction. Fortunately, the modern historical study of the Scriptures is today in a position to serve at this point. We understand better today how a faith arising out of Judaism could bridge the "grand canyons" which divided Jew and Greek, wise man and barbarian, slave and freeman in the ancient world. We understand better how the very nature and possibilities of human community were redefined. Our better understanding of the Christian movement in its origins and in its classic period in the first century sheds light upon the meaning it can have for a disordered world like ours. We have reference here especially to our better recognition today of the sociohistorical character of biblical and Christian revelation and religion. This faith is to be identified not with ideas or even with "religious experience" but with the operation of God in concrete historical circumstances and in men's perennial task of living with one another.

There are today two particular demands upon religion, apart from that of universalism, which must be met if its claims are to be taken seriously. Christianity can meet these demands if it rightly understands itself.

For one thing, the religious answer today dare not expose itself further to the charge of escapism and false otherworldliness. It is not only the Marxists who scorn religion as an opiate and the Nietzscheans who see Christianity as made up of compensatory fictions. The whole trend of our age is against dividing man up into body and soul, and dividing his values up into material and spiritual. Whether we look at psychology, philosophy or aesthetics we find a common repudiation of this severing of flesh and spirit, and theology today joins the chorus. Religious messages that dilate upon man's "soul" and man's "spirit" usually turn out to be ways of evading what is most difficult and most important; namely, how is man as he really is, in his totality, to be served and saved?

If we take account of the disabused realism of our generation we shall see that no facile forms of idealism, no versions of faith which gloss over the creaturely make-up and needs of men, will serve. It is no answer to say that otherworldly faiths have thrived upon disaster and distress. What makes the case different today is that now for long Western society has developed a this-worldly consciousness unique in the annals of civilized men. Evidently this has its drawbacks where materialism takes on its evil aspects of mammon and sensuality. But what is more important is that it is no longer possible for religion and philosophy to satisfy men with "ideals," dreams and merely spiritual satisfactions.

To deal with life where it is really lived today except by sentimentalists, Christianity must offer sound credentials. It must relate itself to the concrete human situation, the social process, and not to the "soul" of the individual apart from his embodied life, and not to the individual man apart from the web of factors that condition him. In this sense religion must be humanistic and materialistic. It is to the point that Archbishop Temple called Christianity the most materialistic of all religions. One of the clearest findings of recent biblical study is that Jew and early Christian made no cleavage between soul and body or between spirit and matter in the sense that many Greeks did.

Our task today is then to offer a faith that redeems and transfigures the flesh and the world. The religious problem is one of man's whole creaturely life, and this life is a social and political life. Evidently religion must also deal with things invisible and with a goal beyond the world. But Christianity, along with Judaism, is unique in its involvement with man's actual mundane experience. The grim tragedies which focus our concern today are tragedies of man-in-the-flesh and of man-in-community, indeed of man-in-the-family, of economic man, and of man-in-war. No religious sedatives or opiates, no religious ecstasies or intoxications, no celebrations on the margin of the day's work, and no cults apart from the general human predicament will offer significant healing, nor will they receive nourishment from the depths of man's ordeal.

But once this is said we must immediately add, in the second place, that the Christian answer today must even go beyond otherworldly faiths in its witness to ultimates. The distinctive function of religion is to offer men authentic knowledge of and contact with God, the fountain of life. Faith today must fulfill its proper role of testifying to first and last things, to Alpha and Omega. The need for this is indicated again by that same disabused tragic vision of life which also rejects all "spiritual" and escapist solutions. Christianity offers just such total and ultimate answers, not as compensatory fictions but as relevant redemption. For men and women initiated into the ordeals of war and totalitarianism, into the hunger and thirst of our dehumanized culture, and into the knowledge of evil that accompanies these, no limited guarantees or partial religious affirmations will suffice. The prevailing disenchantment, the trend toward an acid and sardonic naturalism, call for the kind of total and cosmic witness that the Christian

Gospel daringly makes. The nature of the primal Christian drama was such that on the one hand it was intimately linked with our human circumstance and on the other it lit up the darkness that veiled man's origin and destiny. If this kind of witness, this kind of revelation, is not forthcoming, then not only the personal predicament of the individual in our society but the public predicament of our hour of history will not be illumined, and the available moral energies and incentives will not be set free.

It is true that many men of good will labor constructively today at the task of reconstruction and reconciliation, both inside and outside the religious institutions. These ministries mitigate the legacies of disaster of recent years. But the impasse is deeper, whether in the hearts of men or in the habituated patterns of social attitudes and sentiments. These kinds of mountain obstacles only faith can remove, a world vision and life engagement grounded in God's historical acts and self-revelation. The individual in his actual situation must know himself linked with the historical processes which were so set in motion and in which the new humanity is defined and empowered.

III

Recent gains in biblical study offer themselves providentially in the present conjuncture to meet the special needs of the time as above set forth. In periods of decisive cultural change a significant interplay of learning with other factors is often to be noted. The Reformation presents us with an example pertinent to our own situation. We have reference to the cultivation of the biblical languages, the renewed interest in the biblical text, the revitalized exposition of the Scriptures in the universities instanced by Colet's examination of Paul's epistles at Oxford, and above all the translation of the New and then the Old Testaments from the original tongues into the vernacular by trained scholars like Luther, Tyndal and Coverdale. Other factors such as the recent invention of printing added to the constellation of favoring circumstances which made the Bible live anew and shape the destinies of nations in a new epoch of Western history.

We live today on the verge of a parallel renewal. Convergent factors are at work today on a world scale to carry our civilization through its time of troubles and beyond the outgrown patterns and loyalties which just because they were once precious are today obstacles. Just as at the time of the Reformation so now religious factors interplay with economic, political and technological. Among the religious factors we must include the New Testament scholarship of the nineteenth and twentieth centuries. This movement, which can be adjudged destructive in its results only by those who identify truth with their own dogma, has been of incalculable importance, as Albert Schweitzer recognized. Especially in its investigation of the life of Jesus it has "laid down the conditions and determined the course of the religious thinking of the future." Disillusioning conclusions as to the trustworthiness of the Gospels have been more than compensated by the clarification of our views of the origin and nature of Christianity. Moreover, the work of the last two or three decades has had a markedly constructive phase, opening up a wealth of insights bearing on the distinctiveness of the Hebraic-Christian outlook and its availability to modern thought and need.

Investigation on the part of many scholars has moved from analysis to synthesis, from highly specialized contributory areas and disciplines to central issues and to generalization. This trend has inevitably involved the critic in wider considerations. The historian becomes theologian or calls on the theologian for collaboration.

This constructive phase of scholarship also leads the critic to see his work in its relation to the needs of the church, and to consider the mediation of his findings to the preacher, the religious educator and the layman.

This disposition has been encouraged by the ever clearer recognition that not only the Gospels but all their strata and the underlying oral tradition were transmitted and shaped throughout by the believing, worshiping, witnessing community. As Martin Dibelius has said: "Form criticism reconciles the critic and the church."

The layman often thinks of the Bible as a book that offers a "philosophy" or a set of ideas about God and his attributes; and of Jesus as one whose main contribution was his teachings about God, immortality and the soul. Such ideas are present in the writings, most often implicitly. Modern study focuses attention rather on the "Gospel" or Good News announced in the New Testament, the message or proclamation, not of the divine nature but of the divine action. This "witness" is the primary, typical and controlling feature of the writings, and of the faith of the Apostolic Age. The substance of the message was the congratulatory announcement of the long-awaited salvation as already in course, calling for repentance and faith especially in view of its imminent climax.

Recognition of this common message clarifies the basic unity of the New Testament. The Good News varies, indeed, in respect to the accrediting evidences offered, or the Old Testament attestations, or the details of formulation, but is otherwise a constant. Even the supposed gulf between the Nazarene and the apostle to the Gentile tends to disappear, though Jesus and Paul invoke different aspects of the common message that God has visited his people in grace and judgment.

The relation of the New to the Old Testament appears in a different light when the Bible is seen not as a compendium of evolving religious ideas, which in one sense it is, but rather as the record of a world drama the episodes of whose "plot" are recounted and interpreted.

The significance of what has so far been said will be missed unless it is realized that the New Testament message and faith spring out of concrete historical and community experience. God makes himself known where men really live. Revelation is not first of all meditated through nature, reason or some mystical faculty but through the blood, sweat and tears of the common life. This emphasis on "incarnation" reaches very far. Thus it is not enough to deny that Christ was a myth and to affirm that he was a historical person executed by Pontius Pilate. The point is that Jesus' whole career and its outcome had their matrix in and drew their significance from the social and cultural conflicts of Judaism of the time. The Gospel arose out of the soil of history. We have to do here with a transaction in the public life of men, a drama whose terms were set by long-standing dilemmas in the life and heritage of Israel and its relation to other nations. The operation of God here is to be seen as a renewal of human community and therefore of the stature of man. Revelation is not to be chiefly identified with new religious ideas or with the wonders and miracles which the early Christians naturally invoked in their effort to convey the significance of the message. Such an understanding of the origins of Christianity suggests how mistaken are some efforts today to renew it.

It is true that the concrete historical situation of Israel in the first century involved certain very particular religious conceptions and a heritage of faith which conditioned the work of Jesus and his followers. Recent study continues to emphasize the "eschatological" outlook of Judaism, that is, its expectation of the new age, and that special view of world history which the Old Testament and other Jewish writings evidence. An extraordinary view of the origins and goal of the human story offered the terms in which the redemptive activity of God was set forth in the Gospel. This calls for fuller statement.

Judaism had come to possess an over-all picture of the world process which was of supreme importance to Jesus and the earliest Christians in formulating their message. This picture was so inwoven into the faith of Israel, into its basic assumptions about the world, that it had the character of a life axiom. Central to it was the idea that history had a goal in accordance with the divine purpose, and that this consummation had its antecedents in the acts of God in the past. The whole world story could not be charted then as a circle, a cycle or a spiral, nor, indeed, as an ascending line. Neither, indeed, could it be represented by a jagged line of crests and troughs, but rather as a letter U. Descent and ascent. A fall and a restoration. Lost and found. Paradise Lost and Paradise Regained. The whole history of the world was like the story of the prodigal son or like the story of Joseph.

The picture had its termini in the Creation and the Last Judgment, or more ultimately in the pre-creative purpose of God and the final new age. In the more immediate foreground lay God's choice of Israel, his discipline of that people through historical vicissitudes and deliverances, the deepening sense of the frustration of the covenant, and the quickened appeal of the faithful for the promised salvation. This "plot," this symmetrical design of history appears, indeed, in its clearest form in parts of the New Testament. As the key to the Christ story and the crucial events on which the church is founded, this wider "salvation-history" describes God's dealings with men from beginning to end. The scheme makes clear the connectedness and continuity of the divine action in the world. The unique feature of this religious world view is that it lays such stress on history as the theater of this action, particularly on that stream of history represented by the old and the new Israel. It is in the actuality of the social process, in everyday community life with its drama, conflicts and disasters that God has found and finds opportunity to declare himself. It is especially in the life of Israel that this revelation is forthcoming. But the resulting view of history widens to embrace all mankind, just as it originates and ends in the universal purpose of God for man.

This theology of history, in terms of lost and found, has all the simplicity of a children's tale. We are reminded of a recurrent pattern or plot in old folktales: ordeal and triumph, banishment and restoration, humiliation and glory, feud and reconciliation. The universal appeal in such fables lies in the fact that we think we recognize our own story in them. So it is with the story of Joseph. But the Bible story as a whole refers to a people as though it were one person, or indeed to the whole race. In short, it offers us no less than a simple account of everything.

This framework of creation and redemption has been familiar to us all from childhood, from our first hearing of the story of the seven days of creation and the Garden of Eden, and the stories of Christmas, Easter and the Last Judgment. We may look upon it all now perhaps wistfully as poetry. We may repudiate it as the most dangerous sort of unreality. We may think of its elements as so much exploded myth. We may regret that the times are no longer with us when poets like Milton and composers like Handel could take it seriously. Yet even if we conclude that it is all a mass of fantasy and fiction, we must still reckon with the fact that it has played a prodigious part in the best life of the past. And it may be that at certain moments of self-knowledge we cry out: How strangely this ancient account of man imposes its truth upon us! Even the Greek and the man of the East has his analogous fables, though they have no such relation to genuine history.

For the Jew of Jesus' time the importance of this scheme of history lay in the fact that it offered him a way of making sense of human life. But it is more important to recognize that his loyalties, ideals and hopes were caught up in this mytho-poetic world story, and that Jesus and his first followers had here an incomparable resource for igniting the ardor of their hearers and releasing moral and religious devotion. At the same time the modern interpreter meets here his greatest difficulty, since the truth value of the symbols used is so deeply compromised for us.

Another aspect of Israel's outlook important for early Christianity relates to its conception of man and his make-up, of what a human being is. This too has been highlighted by recent biblical study and has very important bearings today. What it means, in short, is that Israel alone among all the peoples that had ever lived, not excepting Greece and Rome, had advanced to the true idea of the *person*. In the long story of the race Israel alone had produced that kind of human being that can be called truly *personal*, rather than merely individual or civilized. This strikes us as astonishing only because the genius of Greece, particularly, has distracted us from a true assessment. There is no intention here to obscure the "dawn of conscience" whether in Egypt or elsewhere, or the creative human stature evident in Hellas in its great period. Indeed, the meaning of the person comes to the fore more clearly in Vergil's figure of Aeneas than in any of the heroes of Greek history or literature. This is significantly connected with the greater historical sense of the Roman, and Vergil's sense of the calling of his people. Human individuality no doubt takes on personal aspects in all societies. But if we understand the idea of the person and of interpersonal life truly we shall see that it was only in the life of Israel that they emerged or were called forth. Recognition of this will require a rewriting of much of the history of our civilization, a rewriting which has already begun, and constitutes a challenge particularly to our understanding of the humanities. For while modern thought has acknowledged in a formal way the religious and moral contributions of Israel, it has not recognized sufficiently the unique type of human being produced by Israel, and the way in which this type, as person and as community, salvaged the best in the pagan world and shaped the life of the West.

For the Jew man was a unit; he could not be so sharply divided into body and soul, or flesh and spirit, as in Hellenic and Hellenistic thinking. The self of the man was identified with both aspects and centered in his will rather than in his soul or spirit. The Bible, indeed, speaks of man's "soul" or "spirit," but his proper life as a creature included the "body" as an essential aspect. We have here an integral understanding of man as a willing, acting being, and therefore personal in the sense that his life involves not only his "spirit" but his visible temporal expression, and not only his individual consciousness but his social interrelation. This is a realistic view of personal life which commends itself to modern psychology—even though it carries with it the perplexing corollary that life beyond the grave assumes, in some sense, the resurrection of the body. This "psychosomatic" integral view of the person was carried over into Christianity.[3]

This idea of man's constitution goes far to explain the Jewish-Christian view of revelation. If God is to make himself known to man it cannot be through the reason or spirit of man as abstracted from his whole personal life and experience. Such conceptions of religious knowledge, at home in various mystical, ascetic and romantic traditions, belong rather to the certain Greek and Oriental environments. The clarification of this point has led to very significant corollaries in our recent study of Christian origins. The matter must not be overstated. There are valid aspects of Christian experience which are subjective, mystical, "spiritual." Moreover, the Hellenization of Christian thought in the early church inevitably imposed the terms of Greek psychology upon some of the writings of the New Testament and upon the usage of the early Fathers. But such terms are always qualified in their sense by the Hebraic

[3] "The Greek-dualistic anthropology with its conception of the tension between the spiritual and the sensuous . . . is remote. The distinctive trait of man is not the logos, the reason, the spirit. If one poses the question to Christianity as to where it is to be found, the answer can only be: in the will. In any case, existence as man, life as human life, is always understood as a movement-out, a reaching-after, a willing." Rudolf Bultmann, *Das Urchristentum im Rahmen der antiken Religionen* (Zurich, 1949), p. 200. See also W. G. Kümmel, *Das Bild des Menschen im Neuen Testament* (Zurich, 1948).

and early Christian background. It is with the "heart" that man believes unto righteousness, though the knowing faculty and the reasoning faculty are not left out of account. The frequent contrasts of flesh and spirit in Paul's letters mislead the layman in their English translation, for in modern culture the term spirit, in contrast with body or matter, has taken on special connotations. Similarly the term soul in our English Bibles tends to mislead. "What shall man give in exchange for his soul?" (Mark 8:37) in the Authorized Version is more correctly translated, "What can a man give in return for his life?" as in the Revised Standard Version. Except for special cases, Paul, as Bultmann shows, "uses *psyche* (i.e., "soul") altogether in the Old Testament-Jewish tradition; namely, to designate human life, or rather to denote man as a living being." [4]

Just as Paùl does not know the Greek-Hellenistic conception of the immortality of the soul (released from the body), neither does he use *psyche* to designate the seat or the power of the mental life which animates man's matter, as it had become the custom to do among the Greeks.[5]

The point is that God deals with us as personal creatures and as creatures who through their embodied natures are in concrete relationships. The "soul" or the "spirit" can all too easily be thought of in detachment, and its religious emotions or ecstasies can appear to testify to God in escapist and other-worldly terms which may have little relation to man's integral nature and social character. Not so with the embodied personal life envisaged in the prevailing biblical view of man.

Evidently these biblical conceptions will have their diffi-

---

[4] *The Theology of the New Testament* (London: S.C.M. Press, 1951), p. 204.

[5] *Ibid.*, p. 203 f.

culties for many today. In what concerns the dependence of the individual upon the group we seem to recognize crude ideas of tribal solidarity. The psychology, moreover, appears to rest on a prescientific naïveté.

For centuries, under Greek influence, Christian thought has accustomed us to a view which exalts the reason or spirit of man, and one which exalts the free individual, an essential element in our noblest democratic conceptions. These affirmations are surely to be defended, but we should be aware of how easily they can be used to sanction irresponsibility. The Bible warns us that man's "God-like reason," which it recognizes and liberates, is not an autonomous faculty in man but an aspect of his creaturely being and personal responsibility. Similarly the "spirit" of man, which romanticism has rightly affirmed, is warned that its sources are not in nature but in the creator. Again, the biblical idea of the person and his social solidarity humbles our assertion of individual freedom. We are not our own. Nor may we do what we will with our own.

It has become almost axiomatic with us, further, that God deals with us in the "soul" of the individual, and in the sentiments, aspirations and transcendent powers associated with it. Thus we tend to confine religion to the experiences of the soul. Even when we picture to ourselves the religion of the prophets, of Jesus himself and of Paul, we see it in these terms.

We have a romantic picture in mind of Jesus exalted at the fords of the Jordan and of Paul struck down by a vision at the gates of Damascus. In some hour of ecstasy God communicates a divine nature or wisdom to his elect. But the Bible, while it gives due place to the emotions or "religious affections," is concerned with the whole man and therefore speaks of the heart rather than the soul. It is the heart, will, obedience, action, which define the man, and condition the work of God in him and through him. And while the man so understood stands alone before God, yet he is not alone, because God approaches him only through the covenant under which he lives with his fellows.

It is not the biblical picture of man but the Greek picture which is the more "primitive" and inadequate and depersonalizing. Aristotle, indeed, recognized that man was a *social* animal. But with his assumptions he could not see what significance man's social relatedness and his bodily nature have for understanding the divine order in the world. With its depreciation of the body and its inadequate psychology classical thought was specially handicapped in problems of ethics and politics, and fell far short of meeting the need of the city-state and the Roman world.[6]

It should be evident, then, that recent biblical study has important insights to offer in the present dilemma of the Christian faith. Traditional formulas can come to life and receive fresh meaning for the churchman. More important perhaps, ways of stating the perennial message and the distinctiveness of Christianity are available which can be cogent and which will make sense to secularized groups.

We recognize that the Gospel has never rested its final appeal upon its reasonableness as judged by the world's tests. But it is a contrary error to forego all accommodation of it to prevailing conceptions and to think that we can rest its case upon the pure Word of God unmediated and uninterpreted. Today we see this approach in many quarters. The message

[6] Cf. Charles N. Cochrane, *Christianity and Classical Culture* (London: O.U.P. 1944).

in its pristine terms, apart from any adequate translation for modern hearers, has become the theme of a considerable biblical and theological revival. It is one form of what is called neo-orthodoxy, but the term is used so variously today that it has become almost meaningless. We may well hail the biblical and theological revival of these last decades as it centers in a recovery of the basic message of the New Testament, that message which we shall be concerned to clarify in all that follows. But by a pardonable reaction to errors of the past neo-orthodoxy has tended to create a gulf between the Gospel and the world. No doubt there is such a gulf if we have in mind the evil in the world. But there is the false assumption that God's life could come into the world without relating itself genuinely to human circumstance and culture. There is the false assumption that the Word of God could come into the world without relating itself to human words. And while these interpreters hold no doctrine of verbal inspiration of the Scriptures, they nevertheless insist on the unchanged validity today of the particular terms, formulas and conceptions in which the message clothed itself in the first century. If the defense of the Gospel from totalitarianism and secularism requires a retreat upon this kind of a Maginot line, it argues a penury of faith rather than the quickening of faith claimed for the church's resistance to Nazism. Rather we should conclude that the appeal to the Word of God was a true and vital impulse but that it oriented itself to only one limited sector of the task of the church, and is in the process today of modifying its original exaggeration.

Thus the Christian witness will still be hindered unless it can be better related to what, for better or worse, we have come to understand as modern men about history and about man and his needs. Indeed, the meaning of the Word of God may be seriously distorted and its impact impoverished if we allow ourselves in any degree to overlook the human context of its first formulation or the opportunity given us of reinterpreting it in terms of our own culture. The fact is that despite modern scholarship and continued vitality in biblical interpretation, our understanding of the Bible and its conceptions still awaits far-reaching and bold proposals. It is not that we exaggerate the importance of modern ideas nor that we fail to recognize the perennial authority of the Scripture. It is rather that we would shun stereotypes. Older formulas grow wooden. Even where they are cherished and inspiring they blind us to what is significant. To bring the special challenges of our time to the Bible, and to make a bold attempt to reconceive it in terms of our peculiar resources, will mean a truer grasp of it, not only of its relevance to us but of its inmost meaning.

II

the language of faith

And we impart this in words not taught by human
wisdom but taught by the Spirit, interpreting spiritual
truths in spiritual language. 1 Cor. 2:13, r.s.v. margin

I

The words and images of the New Testament seem more and
more to belong to a foreign language and a strange outlook.
The modern speech translations help but even here many of
the key terms and conceptions that go with them appear outmoded and unreal. We need only mention terms like "justification," "Son of Man," "demon," or ideas like those suggested
by the last judgment, ascent into heaven or virgin birth. It is
because our contemporaries are puzzled or impatient with
such features of the canon that we find so many efforts today
to demonstrate the "relevance" of the New Testament or to
urge the "vitality" of the biblical tradition. This problem is
not a new one. Since the seventeenth century the scientific
outlook and historical method have created difficulties for the
believer. The church has had to wrestle with particular issues
such as cosmology, evolution and miracles. Orthodoxy has
given ground at many points and learned much in the process
as to the nature of the biblical writings and their proper interpretation. Injudicious proponents of science and shallow
modernists have for their part often shown themselves to be
in the wrong.

But today the problem takes on a new form and seriousness.

This is partly because new areas of scientific study like psychology have been brought to bear upon the Bible. It is partly because the unsettling conclusions of earlier work have spread to wider circles. But it is also because the difference of the Bible's whole view of the world and of history is recognized today in all its sharpness, and therewith the disparity between its language and symbols and those of the modern mind. This difference is indicated by the increasing use of the term "myth" in various senses to describe the biblical account of reality.

The writers of the New Testament have their own particular way of picturing the world, certainly a pre-Copernican way; also their own way of representing history, a way which the modern historian finds very naïve; and also their own way of portraying the forces heavenly or diabolical with which man is involved, and the manner in which he secures his well-being or salvation. Man, history and the world are all interrelated in the New Testament, of course, and faith deals with all of them. Thus Jesus, Paul and the fourth evangelist employ cosmological conceptions and views of man and history familiar to their respective backgrounds. The religious ideas of Israel play a large part here. The tradition of a three-story universe made up of Sheol, earth and heaven is closely interwoven with the early message. Christ's descent into Sheol, his ascension to heaven, his second coming from heaven are conceived very realistically and may be taken as illustrations of this world picture.

The New Testament's portrayal of the course of history presents us with just as much of a dilemma. Following Oscar Cullmann's diagram [1] there are three periods. First comes the

---

[1] *Christ and Time* (London: S.C.M. Press, 1951), p. 82.

period before the creation, thought of naïvely as an indefinite passage of time. Then comes the period that runs from the creation to the judgment, divided into two parts by the first coming of Christ. Third, there is the period of the new creation, continuing indefinitely and not thought of as a timeless existence. Thus Christ's coming is the center of universal history. He is, moreover, the second Adam in whom a new history begins in the very midst of the period of earthly history. But this human drama has a suprahuman background: the strife of God and Satan, angels and demons; and it leads on to a final cosmic catastrophe in which the hostile powers are definitively overthrown. This whole conception of history is of course closely related to widespread conceptions in the ancient Near East especially Persian and late Jewish. But the New Testament message is so closely interlocked with it that we cannot easily strip it off as an obsolete accompaniment of that message. Christ's significance as the new Adam depends upon the account of the first Adam and the Fall. In the Gospel of John his significance as the Revealer is linked up with the conception of his existence before the creation. Moreover, the cross and resurrection must have their conclusive sequel in the second coming and final judgment.

These conceptions of man and the world have become more and more unreal for hosts of men. When Milton's *Paradise Lost* was written it was possible to assume acquaintance with, and consent to, them. But increasingly since the eighteenth century this great epic has appeared to many to be based upon an alien and outdated ideology. A recent writer, generalizing with regard to the religious crisis of today in Western civilization, speaks of "the smashing of the traditional myth-history" of Christianity.

The new astronomy had undermined confidence in the uniqueness of the Incarnation; the new biology destroyed the symmetry of Christian history which had been designed to explain that Incarnation. Consequently, in the opinion of many men, the entire structure collapsed, and faith in the singleness and purpose of the time-process waned.[2]

Professor Rudolf Bultmann of Marburg has raised these questions in a thoroughgoing way in the course of his work on the New Testament during the last quarter century.[3] As a Christian he is disturbed by the false impression the New Testament makes on many men today. They shrug it off as a collection of writings full of absurdities and fables. His friends, for instance, who were chaplains with the German armies in various parts of Europe, Asia and Africa, reported to him that among soldiers of all ranks and among the peasants of occupied lands and prisoners of war of the enemy peoples, the Christian religion was widely neglected if not scorned, and the Bible looked on as a compendium of myths and legends. Bultmann, of course, was familiar with the similar attitudes toward the Scriptures among intellectuals, artists and the cultivated classes. As a Christian, then, he saw the need of explaining the apparently outdated features in question. As a scholar, and one of the greatest, he knows that the Gospels and Epistles of the New Testament presuppose ideas which we today call unscientific or prescientific, parallels to which can be found in ancient pagan thought and religion. This is not only a matter of ancient cosmology, geology and astronomy. Nor is it only a

[2] Lynn White, "Christian Myth and Christian History," in *Journal of the History of Ideas,* Vol. III, No. 2, April, 1942, p. 155.

[3] Especially *Offenbarung und Heilsgeschehen* (Munich, 1941) cf. *Essays* ch. V (London: S.C.M. Press, 1955); H. W. Bartsch (ed.), *Kerygma und Mythos* (Hamburg, 1948); 2nd ed. 1951. (English ed. *Kerygma and Myth,* London, 1953.) Also: Bartsch (ed.), *Kerygma und Mythos,* 2, Hamburg, 1952.

matter of ancient views of time including the idea of the end of the world. These features have to do only with what we can call the *theater* of salvation. More difficult still for the modern mind are the ideas of the early Christians concerning the divine action that takes place in this theater, the process of salvation itself. The coming of the redeemer from heaven, the incarnation of the Word of God, his atoning death and resurrection, and his reign in the Spirit: the scholar knows that these conceptions also have their parallels in pagan religions. They are traceable to myths of the ancient world, and here the word "myth" is used in quite a different sense from that intended above where the layman talks of "myths and legends." The historian of religion speaks of a myth as a narrative concerning the gods and their relation to the world, without disparaging it as such. It may convey immense significance. Many of them surely did. They were ways in which men offered themselves an account of the world, and profound wisdom often found expression in them. Thus in modified form they could be taken over into the New Testament as vehicles of the Christian witness to salvation. But they are today very strange and constitute a problem.

Bultmann, then, uses the terms "myth" and "mythology" in this sense, not in the scornful sense, of many of the structural features of the New Testament. If we are to make the Gospel relevant for today, he believes, these elements must be stripped off. To preach in these terms is to archaize. On the other hand, we cannot just remove these elements and identify the Gospel with what is left. That is the way of the modernists. The solution is to detach the old-world conceptions but replace them by a modern equivalent, which for him means a presentation of the faith in the framework of a contemporary school of philosophy.

As Bultmann analyzes the matter, the Gospel of the first Christians was formulated in mythological terms in two respects, "formal" and "material." The "formal" myth refers to the cosmological elements that underlie the message—especially the three-story world picture and the idea of a final world catastrophe with the attendant ideas of Satan, demons and angels. Thus the "ascension" of Christ, his "descent" into Sheol, his second coming on the clouds, the dramatic final judgment—all such representations, he holds, are not today believable and must be dismissed. The "material" aspects of the Christian myth refer to the doctrine of the redeemer, his pre-existence, incarnation and redemptive role. Of this Bultmann retains only the crucial underlying conception of the action of God as meaningful today. In his view both mythical aspects, formal and material, must be restated. The mythology is "true" but obsolete. Its removal does not affect the permanent truth of the faith. And this author is ready to supply an interpretation of the Christian faith for the modern world, one which is both timely to our present outlook and faithful to the intent of the early Christian message, especially in its Johannine form.

What concerns us here in this author's thesis is not his proposed solution which has far-reaching constructive value but his honesty in facing the problem.[4] There is simply no gainsaying the fact that the Good News was formulated in terms of

---

[4] Cf. Kendrick Grobel, "Bultmann's Problem of NT Mythology," in *Journal of Biblical Literature*, LXX, II, June, 1951, pp. 99–104, and A. N. Wilder, "Mythology and the New Testament," in *ibid.*, LXIX, II, June, 1950, pp. 113–28. See also Erich Dinkler, *The Journal of Religion*, XXXII, II, April, 1952.

a cosmology, a philosophy of history and a psychology, or of several of each of these, which if taken at face value are inadmissible to thinking men today. For example, the Christian is so familiar with the idea of the Holy Spirit as acting upon the believer or upon the sacramental elements that he hardly stops to consider what is implied, namely, a survival of a highly animistic point of view. Invasion of our bodies or selves by a "spirit" either of God or of Satan is incredible with many today except as a figure of speech, and a Christian apologetic in these terms is under great handicaps. Another sensitive point in Bultmann's argument has to do with the resurrection of Christ. The indispensable truth of this element of the message is maintained, but it can be safeguarded all the better if we recognize the limitations of the early reports.

Though we may follow with sympathy such an examination of the difficulties presented to us by the New Testament symbols and conceptions, we may well examine further the use here of the terms "myth" and "mythology." To be fair to Bultmann, we should note that he recognizes many positive values in the features in question. For the early church they were an indispensable resource in commending its faith. Moreover, the term "myth" is not used here in the popular sense of that which is sheer fiction. Yet when professional historians of religion like this scholar use the term, they do in effect disparage its significance since they emphasize the relativity of this picture language to its culture origins in the remote past. This means that for them the mythology has little inherent truth and that it rapidly grows obsolete. We, for our own part, would emphasize the insight into abiding realities contained in it, and therefore its continuing usefulness in later times. Thus the myth of the creation tells a story which is still true and important. If the modern skeptic is impatient with it or ridicules it, we should correct an elementary misunderstanding of literature on his part and not throw out the myth.

It is to be admitted that distinctions need to be made in the types of mythopoetic material in the New Testament. Much is marginal and much needs to be tested by congruence with the central message.[5] But the fundamental point is that mythology in the sense of imaginative presentation is essential in religion. The language of faith requires it and glories in it. The more vital the faith is the more inevitably its world vision projects itself in such language just as it projects itself in dramatic ritual. When recourse to imaginative vision is abused, correction is called for by tests of sobriety and truth. When the imaginative vehicles become misleading through their dated character, they call for interpretation usually rather than for rejection. But to dismiss "mythology" in favor of the prose of religion is to rationalize something which cannot be rationalized to this degree.

The impulse to rationalize the ancient poetry of faith, to make "myth" reasonable, is notably illustrated by the scholasticism of the medieval church. Dante trusted the poetry of the Bible, while Thomas Aquinas inevitably forfeited something of its truth by formulating it according to an intellectual pattern. Even more clearly, eighteenth-century Christianity, being constitutionally averse to "mythology," would have nothing to do with the profounder images of the Gospel, and arbitrarily disqualified much of the necessary language of faith and there-

[5] See W. G. Kümmel, " Mythische Rede und Heilsgeschehen im Neuen Testament," *Coniectanea Neotestamentica, XI* (Lund und Köpenhamn, 1947), pp. 109–31 ; Regin Prenter, " Mythe et Evangile," *Revue de Theologie et de Philosophie, XXXV,* 1947, pp. 49–67 ; also the critiques of Bultmann's position included in *Kerygma und Mythos, 1* and *2.*

with its substance. For his part Professor Bultmann is aware
of this mistake. He knows that the heart of Christianity is at
stake in the great ancient metaphors and images. He is therefore scrupulous in seeking an adequate translation of them
even as he feels the necessity of abandoning them.[6]

II

There is then no question that a great task of reinterpretation of the Bible and of Christian origins remains to be per-
formed for our time. Jesus' announcement of an imminent
new age and Paul's doctrine of redemption in the cosmic
setting which he gives it are two main examples of teachings
that are alien to us and that cause difficulty. But we must give
further attention to the basic question raised above and that
has to do with the kind of language faith necessarily employs.
Men of our time do not sufficiently appreciate that faith of
any great stature has to have its own kind of rhetoric, its own
kind of vehicle and symbols. When they are confronted with
this kind of language, they are unable to accord it its rights.

Perhaps the chief obstacle here is that men today so often
have forgotten how powerful an experience faith can be. If
they could realize the true dynamics of such a movement of
faith as underlies the New Testament, they would grant that

---

[6] Those familiar with Bultmann's thesis will recognize that we have in
mind here his "existentialist" interpretation of the Gospel. By the use of
Heidegger's categories he offers a modern understanding of the perennial
truth of the New Testament "mythology." The risk here is not that of
the rationalist; it is that of subjectivism. The *shared* apprehension of
reality afforded by the imaginative language of faith tends to be forfeited for a strictly inward and lonely encounter with God. But it is
precisely the dramatization of faith in such language and ritual which
safeguards the solidarity of believers with one another through the centuries. To say this is not to sanction the dogmatizing of the Bible's
mythological elements as found in much systematic theology and in Protestant biblicism.

some such picture language as it so often employs is to be
expected. Even such a secular faith movement as Nazism
couched itself in emotionally-charged symbols and projected
its own reading of history past and future in persuasive fiction
generated out of the intensity of its own drama. The New
Testament's world conceptions were thrown up by a prodigious
impulse of faith—resting indeed upon older traditions, especially upon the long heritage of Israel—and we should expect
to find these conceptions expressed in mythopoetic terms. The
word "faith" is used in various ways in the New Testament,
but we can recognize that when Jesus speaks of the power of
faith and when Paul speaks in his characteristic way of faith,
something momentous is indicated.

Benjamin W. Bacon has used the analogy of the faith of
Jeanne d'Arc to illuminate that of Jesus.

"One believer," says a commentator on Jeanne's story, "is
mightier than a hundred unbelievers." Jeanne, and the Master
on whose name she called with a great cry in her dying agony,
"Jesus," were alike in their appeal to "faith." Whatever victory
the world admits for either was a victory of faith, an indomitable
faith in God cherished in their own souls, a faith infused into the
souls of simple-hearted followers by lives of transparent loyalty
and truth. Thus armed they "subdued kingdoms, wrought righteousness, obtained promises. . . ." [7]

Faith of this kind proceeds from a very deep level. It springs
from the very sources of life itself and with such power that it
carries a man's whole life along with it in its course, and the
destiny of many other men also.

But the faith of Jesus was not only a personal attitude. It
meant also an integrating vision of the world and the world
process. There are immense differences in the level of aware-

[7] *Jesus the Son of God* (New York: Holt, 1930), pp. 40, 41.

ness at which men live. We are not referring here merely to
fluctuations of mood and feeling, or varieties of religious experience, but to radically different ways in which life and the
world are apprehended. With these various perspectives go
corresponding various ways of conceiving all that is and all
that happens. Jesus' picture of the kingdom of God, and all
that goes with it—the judgment and final resurrection, heaven
and hell, Satan and the angels—proceeds out of such a creative vision. Similarly, Paul's picture of human history and
experience, for all its strangeness, takes into account aspects of
human experience to which our modern perspective does not
do justice. It is true that we live in a later, a scientific, era.
But in the New Testament we find ourselves face to face with
a depth of mood, a sense of existence, which transcends our
usual categories. These founders of Christianity were in the
grip of overmastering forces in a critical hour, and they had
advantages for conceiving and interpreting the world which
were unique. A great faith of this kind projects its own vision
upon the world, it makes its own world, and employs a language proper to such experience.[8] Inevitably these conceptions
take us by surprise. The history which such faith construes is
a different history from that which we chronicle. It turns its

8 Cf. Erich Frank, *Philosophical Understanding and Religious Truth*
(London: O.U.P., 1945), p. 90: "Our conception of nature, then, is
not merely an impression of the senses, but is also a projection of our
imagination. . . . It is for this reason that man's sensory picture of the
world is so flexible and varies according to the intellectual presuppositions by which it is determined at various periods of history and in various
schools of thought. We know that the Greek philosophers saw the world
with different eyes from ours, and the conception of nature following
from the latest scientific findings differs considerably from that of even a
few decades ago." What is said here of nature is true also of history,
man and the world generally. New scientific findings, moreover, can be
less significant than other factors in changing or correcting our picture
of things.

spotlight on man and his story from a special angle. Much that we ordinarily concern ourselves with is thrown into the shade, and much that we ordinarily ignore or are hardly aware of is thrown into high relief. Poetry does this too, but religious faith does it supremely. Inevitably the language employed by faith of this kind, the vehicle of its expression, will have a special character.

We should be ready to recognize that our habitual vision of the world may be very partial and faulty. Professor Toynbee states this effectively.

The universe as we see it through contemporary Western eyes is not the true picture of the universe as it is. In the perspective even of a distant future in this world, it will probably come to seem fantastically out of focus. . . . This illusion is the greatest obstacle to our salvation even on the secular plane of life.[9]

Thus our modern cosmogony, cosmology and history may have corrected many errors, but we may at the same time have lost more than we have gained if we relegate entirely the biblical mythological accounts of the world in favor of more shallow ones.

It should be noted that we are not trying to justify all the fantastic and bizarre myths that the religious consciousness has produced, nor to assert the literal truth of the language of faith, nor to exempt it from critical examination. Much religious symbol, many biblical symbols, are rightly suspect. But we are saying that great faiths must have a special kind of language and that the Christian faith *has* a special kind of language which in many particulars cannot be dispensed with or replaced.

[9] *Christianity and Civilization* (London: S.C.M. Press, 1940) cf. in *Civilization on Trial* (London: O.U.P., 1948).

D

Thus the right of faith to its own kind of language grows clear as soon as we bring vividly to mind the elemental and sometimes catastrophic power that accompanies its birth. And all great faith, even when it has channeled itself in institutions and doctrines, continues to evidence these primal dynamics and therefore to insist on extraordinary formulation. Thus faith calls forth new doxologies and liturgies, new spirituals and poems, new confessions and propaganda forms which seem in one respect or another extravagant or naïve, audacious or ingenious, otherworldly or even obscurantist. But faith will insist on the legitimacy of its Gospel and of the special grammar of faith and rhetoric of faith. Faith will and must be intransigent in these matters, however willing it will be to go half way to make itself intelligible. It is talking about and singing about things it has seen and heard, tasted and handled. Its knowledge if it be Christian rests also in sociohistorical experience; it roots deeply in the everyday life of men and nations. This is no mere excitement of the mind or intoxication of the soul, no cosmic consciousness or private mysticism. Genuine faith of this kind must remain intransigent where common sense or reason presumes too much with regard to it. Our reach here immeasurably transcends our grasp. The essential in faith is confused and stultified if we fail to recognize this disparity. To deny or minimize the abiding element of mystery and awe in the religious life is to forfeit that life itself. It follows also that the language, symbols and rites of religion have their own autonomy.[10]

[10] What Luther wrote with regard to the ancient languages holds true for the language of faith generally: "We shall not retain the Gospel without the languages [Hebrew, Greek, Latin]. . . . The languages are the scabbard in which is the word of the Spirit; they are the tabernacle in which this piece of jewelry is carried about; they are the cup in which this drink is contained. . . ."

Once this authority of the wisdom and language of faith is admitted, it is immediately to be granted that they are both amenable to criticism, and must everlastingly be retested by the Spirit and put to the proof of reason. In the last analysis the deliverances of faith are only effectively challenged or modified by faith itself, or destroyed by unfaith. But reason can and should play its part. It is one of the means by which we may test how far faith deals honestly with all human experience, and how far it is consistent with itself. The working of faith and the affirmations of faith, together with its Scriptures, must be everlastingly put to the proof not only in the light of our own religious experience, but also in the light of common sense, reason, conscience and science so far as they can be brought to bear. There remains, however, for the believer a real gulf between what he most deeply apprehends by all the faculties of his being and what he can know by systematic means, and this disparity carries over into the world picture that results and the language with which it is communicated.

III

In the First Epistle to the Corinthians Paul is led to make a contrast between wisdom of a worldly kind and the wisdom of God and of the Gospel, revealed to us through the Spirit.

Now we have received not the spirit of the world, but the Spirit which is from God, that we might understand the gifts bestowed on us by God. *And we impart this in words not taught by human wisdom but taught by the Spirit, interpreting spiritual truths in spiritual language.* [1 Cor. 2:12–13, R.S.V., margin.]

Paul is under fire in the Corinthian Church because his furniture of religious ideas, his counters in debate and his rhetoric in presentation do not meet the standards of religious discussion in Hellenistic circles. Paul is challenged by his sophisticated converts from paganism to use their categories of knowledge and moral philosophy and the accomplished arts of eloquence which gave them such delight. But Paul cannot do this. This approach will not reach the heart or engage the whole man. Neither will it take into account the world in its totality. He does, indeed, go far to meet them on their own ground, using conceptions and symbols drawn from the syncretism of the period, but his message is finally based on what is to them a cruder, more naïve ideology. He had to resort finally not to Hellenistic speculation but to the whole biblical world story: creation, fall, atonement, consummation. This picture of the world drama seemed naïve and unscientific and, as we say, superstitious to pagans of that day and even to many Gentile Christians.[11] But the point is that some such symbolic story of the whole of human existence and destiny was necessary if the early Christian faith in its full scope was to be conveyed. In the light of the divine action the world was unified for the believers; they could be sure it hung together, from Alpha to Omega. This understanding required a world picture and world story different from the shallower conceptions of Hellenistic theosophy. Even when Paul utilized the gnostic mythology of the Heavenly Man or Revealer, this "wisdom of man" was, as we shall see, recast in terms of the "wisdom of God" by being radically reshaped under the influence of Jewish eschatology and the historical realism of

[11] Cf. E. C. Colwell, *John Defends the Gospel* (New York: Harper, 1936), pp. 95–101. "The Christian doctrine of a future judgment and punishment was naturally seized upon as evidence that Christianity was a superstition" (p. 95).

the early Christian message. For the absence of a doctrine of creation in gnosticism and its dualism of spirit and flesh meant that a great part of existence fell outside the control of God or any possibility of redemption.

A chief difficulty in the Bible for modern men, indeed, arises out of its pretension to give a comprehensive view of the whole of existence. It is precisely those elements in its outlook which pretend to universality which make the most difficulty: the beginning and end of the world—i.e., creation and eschatology and the centrality of Israel, Christ and the church for the whole race. The skeptic rejects these doctrines from the outset as mere myths, no more or less true than the myths that have arisen in other peoples and other regions. Even Christians today tend to relinquish just these aspects of their faith, these claims of the Gospel to deal with cosmic and final matters and with Christ viewed in these total perspectives.

Many of us today, unfortunately, are content with a more modest and a more humanistic outlook. We do not deny necessarily that light is thrown upon ultimates by our version of faith, but we feel constrained to leave such matters in uncertainty. We cut down the field of vision and direct the beam of faith upon what we consider to be more immediate concerns. In plain language this means that we in effect set aside the assurance that God is the one governor of the world and that there is a single overruling power and purpose in all that happens. We are hardly able, for example, to take confidently, in their full sense, such sublime ascriptions as this one in Jude: "To the only God, our Savior . . . be glory, majesty, dominion, and authority, before all time and now and for ever." Such a faith may be a matter of hope or liturgical convention to us, but not of settled conviction. We find too many evidences that the world has impersonal and meaningless aspects.

It is connected with these hesitations that we also in various ways leave in abeyance the conviction that in Christ we have the definite disclosure of this one God and his purpose. We are content to find in him an incomparable clue to the possibilities of living, and one whose own faith in God points us to what we can aspire to share. We also are inclined to set aside belief in life after death and in a new creation to come. To repeat, it is just these aspects of the Bible which deal with the greater perspectives, with the total view of the world, which make the most trouble for men today. But it is just these grand lines of the biblical faith which necessarily are couched in a special language and in symbolic terms. Of these spiritual things the New Testament speaks in spiritual language. But we should not let our difficulties with the idiom stand in the way of the greater faith itself.

For note that what we retain of our Christian faith in the reduced field of vision loses its cogency and grounding when taken by itself. Take away the larger frame of reference and the meaning of the rest disappears. Remove the circumference of a circle and its center vanishes. The "meaning" or importance of Jesus of Nazareth fades very rapidly if his life is not seen in relation to ultimates and if his cross is not located at the crossroads of history.

The message of the Son of God who dies upon the cross, of a God who transcends history and is yet in history, who condemns and judges sin and yet suffers with and for the sinner, this message is the truth about life. It cannot be stated without deceptions but the truths which seek to avoid the deceptions are immeasurably less profound. Compared to this Christ who died for men's sins upon the cross, Jesus, the good man who tells all men to be good, is more solidly historical. But he is the bearer of no more than a pale truism.[12]

No pattern for life can pretend to do for us what religion should do unless it offers us a view of the whole, deals with first and last things, and gives us assured communion with God the Stranger of Job who is at the same time the God and Father of Jesus Christ.

We find a helpful analogy to the world-integrating power of faith in the peculiar faculty of the poet. It has often been pointed out that the imaginative vision of the poet not only sees particulars with intense vividness but triumphs over multiplicity and unrelatedness, and reconciles disparate elements of experience into organic wholeness. The contingent, the fragmentary, the incoherent, fall into a pattern that is not artificial but recognized as the true and the meaningful. And we are related to the whole.

> . . . poetry, to revert to Donne's great phrase, seeks either to "contract the immensities" and so to communicate them, or to induce in us a state in which, as Mr. Bowra says, "we feel that we are the centre, if not of the universe, at least of some enormous scheme, and that anything we do or that happens to us is pregnant with huge issues." [13]

As the same writer adds, "Art is 'news of reality' expressed in symbols, joys, incantations, enchantments, and the age that cannot read it fails to synthetize its disparate experiences."

The dramatist does this also, working especially with moral actions, conflict and their resolution. The great fables and myths of the peoples sum up large aspects of experience,

[12] Reinhold Niebuhr, *Beyond Tragedy* (London: Nisbet, 1937), p. 3.
[13] "The Heritage of Symbolism," in *Times Literary Supplement*, London, March 13, 1943.

gathering up blind circumstances and incoherent elements into a revealing pattern.[14] It is the peculiar prerogative of faith to carry this out to ultimates. This it accomplishes likewise by still profounder imaginative and spiritual insight, resolving the anomalies and contradictions of the world as a whole. Where such universal perspectives are involved it is evident that we are carried beyond the scope of the poet. This ultimate kind of insight is occasioned by personal and communal wrestling with life, and by the impact of God thus mediated. Moral-historical circumstances furnish the travail and awareness in which this kind of revelation emerges, binding together past, present and future, and linking heaven and earth.

IV

The great faith impulse behind Christianity arose in and through Jesus of Nazareth. This event had its context in the faith of Israel, a faith granted to Israel and won by Israel through vicissitudes linked with those of all mankind in common human experience. Jesus' own life drama and the experience of his followers with him and through him released an incomparable power. This power was creative both in life and in thought. Here it was that the finger of God touched the world as though in a new day of creation. It was as though a spark had been struck between heaven and earth which gave the first community a new and blinding light on existence and which changed the face of the world. Jesus' career and teaching in that critical hour of Israel's history offered the circumstance, but it was the whole drama and fate of Jesus, read in the light of the Scriptures, which set off the spark.

[14] Cf. Santayana, work cited: cf. infra p. 70, *op. cit.*, p. 173: "*La fonction fabulatrice:* which is not idle dreaming; but dramatic divination of potentialities latent in human nature."

Professor John Knox in his book, *On the Meaning of Christ,* defines the Christ event in an illuminating way. In summing up he says:

It was recognized that [this event] has no absolute outer limits except those of history itself, but that it belongs in a special sense to the Hebrew-Jewish-Christian stream, and that it is, more particularly, the central and decisive moment in that historical movement. This moment is not a single happening, but a cluster of inseparable and mutually inter-dependent elements, which might be summed up in the words, "Jesus and all that happened in connection with him." It was through this event *as a whole,* rather than through anything outside of it or any element or combination of elements within it, that the revelation which is the source of what is most distinctive and precious in our own spiritual life took place.[15]

This whole transaction, then, mediated the revelation and the mighty impulse of faith. This spark set off a conflagration. The dazzling light inevitably threw in the shade men's habitual life and outlook. Hence the great antinomies of the Gospel. The New Testament speaks of darkness and light, the temporal and the eternal, death and life. The ends of life were grasped with utmost clarity; the glory before, within and beyond the world was disclosed in glistering radiance. Our life in time was assigned immeasurable significance, since it was seen in its ultimate context. Here is the basis of all life affirmation in Christianity. But at the same time life was swallowed up in immortality. Is it a matter of surprise that the Christian has ever since maintained a detachment from the created order glimpsed as it had been in the livid light of eclipse?

> Flame burst out of a secret pit
> Crushing the world with such a light
> The day sky fell to moonless black,

15 New York: Scribner, 1947, pp. 42, 43.

The kingly sun to hateful night
For those, once seeing, turning back:
For love so hates mortality,
Which is the providence of life,
She will not let it blessed be
But curses it with mortal strife. . . .
Who would come back is turned a fiend
Instructed by the fiery dead.

This poem of Allen Tate's [16] well suggests the overwhelming shock that the cross and the whole revealing event brought to common views of life, whether Jewish or Greek. It also suggests vividly and credibly not only the judgment on life brought by the vision, but also the transcendent perspectives opened up.

The terms in which the Good News was first declared were Jewish terms. Faith found its appropriate language close at hand. God's present working lit up his working in the past and in the future. Israel's heritage offered the terms for this understanding. It had its story of how the world began and of how the world should end and the meaning of the whole process. The new event confirmed this symmetrical picture of history and threw new light upon it.

Thus the New Testament, for its larger faith that the world from first to last lies in the providence of God the Creator and under his overruling, employed the world picture and the world story of Israel, assumed by Jesus himself in all his teaching. This world story which, indeed, had its various versions and differences of detail, began with creation and ran through the calling and proving of Israel, the coming of the Messiah and the New Israel, on to the judgment and the new creation.

[16] "The Cross," in *Poems: 1928–1931*, p. 7. (Copyright, 1931, 1932, by Charles Scribner's Sons. Used by permission.)

This story had elements that could be called historical and others that were nonhistorical. Yet for the believer no part was mere chronicle; sober narrative and heavenly transactions belonged alike to this salvation drama.

It is with this world story and its different elements that much of our modern difficulty lies. Already in the New Testament Christians were restating various parts of the message. But let us recognize one important thing. *Some* picture of the whole world story is necessary for the Christian faith. No great gaps of meaninglessness can be left. For the church there was such illumination in Christ that light from him shone back upon the past and even on origins and forward into the future and even upon the last things. And conversely the full significance of God's work in Christ could only be perceived in the light of God's earlier leadings and promises. To affirm these larger insights of faith the early Christians could only employ mythopoetic statement. We ourselves are under the same necessity.

NOTE: Truth and Religious Symbols

All that we have said in Chapter II raises the basic question of the cognitive value of religious symbols and myth, of how far they embody and communicate truth. It is not enough to insist that faith must use this kind of language. There remains the question of how far such language embodies knowledge and what kind of knowledge. This is an issue which is passionately discussed today not only in theology but in its corresponding aspects in aesthetics. Difficulties and confusions arise here especially because we do not first take account of the immense variety of uses and levels of figurative terminology and of the wide disparities in content and occasion of myth understood in its more general sense. One barrier to understanding arises out of the long use of the terms "myth" or "mythology" in a pejorative sense, as though such material was by definition untrue or fanciful. But the chief obstacle to the proper validation of religious myth and all cognate mythopoetic portrayals of life and history is the stultifying axiom that genuine truth or insight or wisdom must be limited to that which can be stated in discursive prose, in denotative language stripped as far as possible of all connotative suggestion, in "clear ideas," in short, in statement or description of a scientific character.

Yet the proponents of this thesis are increasingly uncomfortable since students of semantics and of science itself have pointed out the symbolic character and fluidity of even the most objective terms and discourse. But such demonstration avails little with those whose whole outlook has been shaped by modern positivism and scientism, or whose inner life has been deprived of affective and imaginative richness. Since, however, human nature itself forbids any such reduction as is here postulated it follows that the modern mind has to recognize the role of the imagination in some degree. The grudging and condescending acknowledgment of such activities of the mind and spirit takes various forms depending on the type or scope of symbolic expression, artistic or religious. All such expressions, however, have this in common—so it is alleged—that they are fiction and irrelevant to the search for true knowledge. They are indexes or "flags" of subjective emotion and thus illuminate if anything the artist or believer rather than any reality which they may seem to report. Where large cultural or cosmogonic myth is concerned, attention is drawn to the childish character of the accounts and the relativity of the conceptions to the circumstances of the tribe or people shaping such fables. The only area where symbol and myth are taken very seriously by the scientific mind is in connection with depth psychology. It should be added that anthropology assigns a pragmatic value to tribal myth. The social delusions in question, it is admitted, further the cohesion of the group.

The denial of the truth value or representational function of symbols and myths is related to the general divorce of intellect and imagination, of sense and sensibility, since the seventeenth century. Systematic scientific discourse alone has benefited by this divorce. Deprived of their proper relation to reason, all expressions of the emotional and imaginative life whether artistic, literary or religious have tended to take on the character of sentimentality or unreality. The function of poetry, for example, has been basically distorted in our period by this split: poets either maiming themselves by feeling obliged to bow to the empirical presuppositions, or, in defense against them, conceiving of their task esoterically as altogether irrational. In theology the same two alternatives have appeared. Theology could conform itself to the reductionist outlook. Or it could commit itself to a defiant espousal of revelation and its dogmatic mythological vehicles without attempting to bridge the gulf. In dealing with the Scriptures, modern interpretation tends similarly either to evacuate its mythological world picture and world story of any truth value and reduce the biblical faith to a residue of general religious or moral ideas, or to authenticate the same as revealed truth, insisting that the "myth" of the Bible is *sui generis,* and not to be read or tested in accordance with the laws of either reason or imagination which, however, apply here as elsewhere.

What is first of all needed is that the complexity of the matter be admitted. Excessive claims should not be made for the truth of symbolic statements nor should the indubitable truth of one instance or kind of symbol be involved to cover the error of another. Nor, on the other hand, should the range and subtlety of human understanding and statement be canceled out by a reductive rationalism. Fortunately, the reaction to such excesses is making itself widely heard today not only in philosophy and semantics, but in aesthetics and theology. The limitations of scientific discourse whether for the grasp of experience or the needs of the common man are being recognized anew.

Men cannot meet the vicissitudes of fortune, the facts of human injustice and of natural inequality, the perplexities and complexities of the relation between the community and the individual, the tragedy of error and guilt, the manifold conflicts and contrasts of human history, and especially of his finite life and his infinite aspirations, without that ultimate knowledge which is barred to the thinking mind, to the inquiry of scientific and metaphysical reason. . . .
This knowledge should be granted to man for moral and spiritual guidance. But for this purpose, it should not be rational, but so fashioned that every man can comprehend it, that is to say, it should be imaginative. The insolubility of the ultimate problem and the exigency of the practical purpose unite thus in the postulate of religious imagination. . . .[17]

We can agree with this statement of Richard J. Kroner though his claim that this kind of knowledge "should not be rational" and is "barred to the thinking mind" is open to misunderstanding. There is no necessary contradiction between the "rational" and the "imaginative."

[17] Richard J. Kroner, "On the Religious Imagination," in *Perspectives on a Troubled Decade: Science, Philosophy and Religion, 1939–1949,* Lyman Bryson (ed.), *et al.* Tenth Symposium (New York: Harper, 1950), pp. 606–7.

We can best characterize the symbolic language of the New Testament and justify its truth value if we first distinguish certain relevant terms and indicate their relation to our subject matter.

By the imagination we mean that synthesizing function of the mind in dealing with experience at all levels whereby we objectify for ourselves realities with regard to which we have rather clues than controlled evidence. The operation of the imagination includes both perception and creation, but the creative operation here is not fanciful, being controlled both by the objectivity of what is sensed and by the need to relate it to our previous knowledge or apprehensions. What Eichrodt says here with regard to the anthropomorphic traits in the biblical picture of God is to the point.

The immediate nearness and reality of God (obscured in more spiritualizing conceptions) comes to the fore in Old Testament revelation and thus compels the clothing of the divine presence in human form.

Yet, as he continues, the metaphorical rather than realistic character of such traits is evident in the fact that the art of the representation is such as to veil the Deity rather than to describe him.[18] Similarly with regard to the employment of the symbol of fire in the representation of the Deity:

It is idle to dispute as to whether in Israel men thought that they actually saw God in such natural phenomena or whether the symbolism indicated an exceptional kind of "seeing" or recognition of God as in a picture.

[18] *Theologie des Alten Testament,* Vol. II (Leipzig, 1939), pp. 4, 5. The same factors operate in the portrayal of Krishna-Arjuna in the Bagavad Gita. See D G. Mukerji, *The Song of God* (New York: Dutton, 1931), pp. 101, 102 in which the cosmic transcendence of the Deity is related to his human incarnation.

Popular thinking makes no such hair-splitting theological distinctions. What emerges from the naïve language is a testimony that the seeing of Gòd was something indisputably real. That God's glory was felt to be properly indescribable is shown by the fact that any attempt to describe his face or form more particularly is altogether absent.[19]

Such "symbol" then means any figure, metaphor or correlative for a reality to be conveyed, especially for elusive, subtle or complex realities and experience not amendable to description or denotation. If we speak of "symbolic discourse" more generally we have in mind more extended units of figurative and pictorial matter; the summation of larger aspects of experience under an extended figure or related figures; discourse charged with tropes and connotative terms.

The New Testament is, of course, full of such symbol and mythopoetical language from beginning to end, from the single detail or metaphor through the parable, allegory, extended trope, legend (in the sense of hagiographic account), to mythical narrative (theophany, etc.), to all-encompassing world myth. The question of the validity or historicity of particular elements is not prejudiced by this general characterization. The point is that the New Testament uses figurative representation as do all saga, epic, sacred books and poetry. Most of this is old and familiar imagery and motif, weighted with meaning through generations, evocative and reproductive of older experience, sentiments and loyalties. Culture and faith live upon just such "generic signs." The dense richness of such symbols, their role in the life of the imagination, and their importance for communication and for social cohesion and tradi-

[19] *Ibid.*, p. 3. For a striking use of the symbolism of fire in suggesting the temple, throne and glory of God see Enoch 14:15-24.

tion is well suggested in the following passage by Professor Milton C. Nahm which is primarily concerned with the arts. After referring to the symbols of the "leader" and that of "light," he writes:

> But one might have ranged afar, to make the point the clearer, among the primordial images which become the classic symbols for art, simply because art revives
>
> > The fair humanities of old religion,
> > The Power, the Beauty, and the Majesty.

And these images live, not in the "faith of reason" but in the life of feeling which is, in part, recognitive and reproductive. Art gains familiarity because of this and the arts display the principle in the recurrence of symbols—symbols of the hunt and the chase, of danger and vengeance, chicanery, death, old age, change, tales of marriage of spring and winter, the passage of time and of the seasons, chance and love, the ladder and the tree of life, the isles of the blest, the demons and the werewolves of a hundred Beowulfs and Homers, tales of horror, the storied fables of the beneficence of warm sun and soft rain, of the mating of earth and heaven, the havoc of storm, hurricane and earthquake, of plague, pestilence, starvation and war. From this I concluded that by the relation of feeling to generic signs we search for communication and its means only to find them "tumbling at our feet" in the permanent record of feelings which men symbolize in their art.[20]

Many of these "signs" or motifs appear in the Old Testament and some are taken up thence into the New. Imaginative religious literature just because of its human setting and relevance is full of such associative cultural symbol. The Gospels, the Acts of the Apostles, the Epistles and, evidently, the Apocalypse testify to a corresponding exploitation of elements

[20] Milton C. Nahm, "Art as One the Bridges of Cultural Understanding: Retrospect and Prospect": Tenth Conference on Science, Philosophy and Religion, in *op. cit.*, pp. 763–64.

E

from a long past. With such folk themes and imagery as
the following the revealing events of God's action in the
Gospel are presented and interpreted: the speech of Deity, the
theophany, the contest of God and Satan, Paradise, the angelic
hierarchy, the birth of the divine child, the water of life, the
New Jerusalem, the celestial court, the underworld, the (cosmic) vine, the primal man, the descent of the Light Bringer.
Such a list could be extended. Such symbols represent the
"available past" which poet but also prophet and apostle draw
upon. At this point we are first of all defending the indispensable role and validity of such imaginative material. At no
level can human society forego it. The question of truth cannot be simply answered where such diverse elements are in
view. But we may emphasize one aspect of the question. The
long-continued vitality of many such symbols argues one kind
of objectivity (if not the objectivity of a scientific proposition,
yet equally significant), namely, that of the unaltering human
sentiments so served. There must be an objective order of experience, of reality in this sense, with which the imaginative
statements correspond, thus acquiring a degree or kind of
"truth." A philosopher like Santayana carries this thesis very
far, though in what concerns the supreme Christological symbol he fails to connect adequately this type of "truth" with
the historical person of Jesus. But the cognitive value of the
symbols often has another aspect, and this appears especially
in connection with myth.

In the narrower sense a myth is a story concerning divine
beings especially in their dealings with man and nature: thus
the myths of Prometheus, of the creation, and of Paradise and
the Fall. Myths can be distinguished by their real subject matter, i.e., the area of experience out of which they arise and

which they objectify. Some myths, at least originally, arose out of man's observation of, and concern with, the cycles of nature, whether of celestial phenomena or of earth's fertility. Some relate to the primary relations of the family: man and woman, parent and child. Some record ancient culture crises, the transition to agricultural life or the use of fire or new tools. The New Testament itself contains residues and transformations of such nature and culture myths. The Apocalypse utilizes ancient cosmological myth. Fertility myth absorbed into the later mystery cults makes through them or through contemporary syncretism an indirect impression upon Christology and the sacraments. The Good Shepherd, the vine, the man from heaven, carried general mythical associations and corresponding appeal for men of the Hellenistic world.

World historical myth requires special attention. Here we have more universal stories or pictures of the total world process or large aspects of it: the conflict of light and darkness, of order and chaos; cycles of creation and destruction; or, as in the New Testament particularly, creation, fall, restoration and consummation. Here we encounter the theology of history or world plot assumed by Jesus and the early church. Late Judaism and early Christianity drew especially here upon cosmogonic and eschatological myth deriving from Persia and Babylonia, reshaping it to accord with the moral insights developed in Israel. Early Christianity also utilized, in conjunction with this, myth of gnostic character at hand in the syncretism of the time, likewise representing an impressive dramatization of human destiny and serving as a vehicle for the sense of existence of multitudes of souls through many generations.

Justification for the resort to such vehicles for the interpretation of history is tellingly presented by A. J. Toynbee. This author reverts to the truth of what he calls "fiction" or "mythology" at numerous points. He recalls Aristotle's statement in connection with the Greek drama that "fiction is truer and more philosophical than history." Here Toynbee adds:

The form of artistic creation and expression called fiction is the only technique that can be employed or is worth employing [in dealing with certain kinds of data]. . . . In such circumstances the data cannot be significantly expressed except in some notation which gives an intuition of the infinite in finite terms; and such a notation is fiction.[21]

Toynbee has in mind not only such art forms as the Greek tragedies and the novels of Dostoevski but also religious narratives like those of the creation and the fall in Genesis. Mythology, he says, is

a primitive form of apprehension and expression in which—as in fairy tales listened to by children or in dreams dreamt by sophisticated adults—the line between fact and fiction is left undrawn.[22]

He continues by insisting that written history has to use such mythology or fiction whenever it would become really significant. In a major feature of his inquiry, the attempt to explain the rise of great civilizations, he recognizes the inadequacy of strictly scientific procedure and turns to mythology as Plato did in dealing with matters bordering on the ultimate.

The dispute as to the cognitive value of myth, its character as a vehicle of truth, is the same dispute as appears in the field of art between the expressionists (e.g., Croce) and the representationalists or symbolists. A moment's attention here will clarify and corroborate our thesis. For the expressionist holds

[21] *A Study of History.* Abridgement of Volumes I–VI by D. C. Somervell (London: O.U.P., 1947), pp. 40–46.
[22] *Ibid.*, p. 44.

that art (here substitute "myth") "tells no story" as to any objective order of things. The work of art (or the myth) if it be an index of anything is one only of subjective intensities and excitements. So R. G. Collingwood describes the aesthetic life as an autonomous activity which "arises from within . . . and is not a specific reaction to a stimulus proceeding from a specific type of external object." [23] Similarly for many anthropologists the whole complex of art, ritual and myth of an Indian tribe is thought of as wholly relative to their peculiar "nature-society-personality integrate," the myth having no objective truth content but simply serving a cultural or survival need.

The difficulty with all such views is that the imagination is thought of as acting *in abstracto*. First of all it is to be insisted that the aesthetic feeling is inseparable from the symbols employed and that these symbols have very concrete reference to shared human experience of objects, events, incidents, etc. Thus the work of imagination is more than expression, it is communication.[24] But it is also representation, for the signs and symbols in question constitute a notation of reality, however different in kind from that of science. Another way to put this is to say that as there is no pure emotion without some element of perception, so there are no symbols without some element of cognition and statement.

Myth, then, like art, offers a report of the world, "news of reality." The importance of the truth represented, or the proportion of truth to error, depends upon the experience and wisdom of those who shaped the myth. The chief integrating symbols of the Bible convey real meaning and interpretative

23 *The Principles of Art* (London: O.U.P., 1938), p. 40.
24 Cf. Nahm, *op. cit.*, pp. 763.

insight. They rose out of costly moral experience and were subject to the corrections of that experience. They were chiefly shaped by spokesmen and prophets whose insight is confirmed by their lives. They received negative confirmation by the sterility of opposing ideals, and positive confirmation by the amazing fruitfulness they manifested in history. In the post-biblical period they communicated a world vision which long served as the framework and setting of the moral vitality of Europe, despite the alienness of their formulation. For such reasons we must assign truth value to the picture language of Christian faith. At the same time we must be careful to dissociate this validation of biblical myth from one to which men in the Platonic tradition are often tempted. For them the myths represent universal ideas or ideals with little attachment to the historical process. We must avoid all such idealism here, represented recently by Santayana's striking study of the idea of Christ in the Gospels.[25]

But there are immense differences in the kind and quality of truth mediated by different myths. The myth of the Bible has a very different genesis and character from that of Greece, for example. Here we have to do not with representations of the cycles of the seasons nor of the fertility of nature, nor of man's psychological constants, nor of ancient ethnic and cultural crises, though these may have been taken up into it in various ways and though these often have their profound meaning. The biblical myth is more general, more important and more true because it arose out of a society living at an increasingly *personal* level. It is particularly in its moral concern and in its

[25] George Santayana, *The Idea of Christ in the Gospels, or God in Man* (New York: Scribner, 1946). Note, however, this writer's defense of the metaphors and anthropomorphisms of the poets and the Bible, p. 177. His assumption throughout is that myth conveys truth.

related view of creation, history, time and judgment that its differentia appear. To speak of it as myth except with the greatest caution is therefore misleading.[26]

[26] Nicholas Berdyaev in his volume, *Esprit et liberté* (Paris: Editions, "Je sers," 1935), devotes a chapter (pp. 73–106) to "Symbole, mythe et dogme." In section IV (pp. 89–95) he states very impressively, though in the context of his own theology, the truth value and indispensability of myth in religion and philosophy. "The myth is a concrete narrative which has engraved itself in the language, memory and creation of a people, in which are expressed the primal events and phenomena of the spiritual life, symbolized in the natural world" (p. 90). He illustrates by the myths of Prometheus, Dionysus and the Fall. His chief criticism is directed against the modern view of myth as a mere projection of psychic experience or religious sentiment. Myths are ontological in their origin; they reflect the divine life, "the depth of being" known in spiritual experience. One can add that the world symbol of the Bible reflects peculiarly the moral aspect of our ultimate being; it is shaped by the experience of the heart and the conscience, and not only of the psyche.

Biblical symbol can be contrasted with Greek myth in another way. The Greek myths deal always with limited forces, limited agents. Even the gods are limited by fate or necessity or fortune. In the central "myth" of Christianity God is omnipotent. There are no remainders beyond his control, whether of inertia or hostility.

III

the proclamation of jesus

The kingdom of God is at hand; repent, and believe
in the gospel.   MARK 1:15

I

Our first chapters have prepared the ground for attention now
to several various expressions of the New Testament faith and
to the problem of relevance as it arises with regard to each.
We shall try to carry over into each of these successive studies
what was there emphasized. We drew attention to the extraordinary dynamics of the primitive Christian faith and to the
special vision of life that inevitably resulted. We noted that
this faith made bold to deal with the ultimate mysteries of our
human lot. To do so it had to borrow or create a special language; as a matter of fact, it availed itself of a whole body of
images drawn from the faith of Israel. All that had to do with
Jesus, especially his cross and triumph, took on meaning in
connection with Israel's memories and hopes.

We turn first, then, to the message of Jesus of Nazareth as
the initial expression of that wave of faith which manifests
itself in the entire New Testament and in Christianity down to
our own day. We may anticipate here by saying that we find
no such gulf between the faith of Jesus and that of the primitive church or of Paul as is often claimed. This is an old
debate. The chief difference lies in the fact that the apostles
gave their witness after the first Easter day. They therefore
directed supreme attention to the resurrection of Christ. They

also were led to explore further the meaning of his life and death and to interpret his person in ways that were far from his own thought. But what is important to keep clear is the agreement. The apostles and later writers agree with Jesus in a common testimony to the present salvation, to the new thing that God has wrought and that is coming to pass. Here Jesus and his followers agree also in their common appeal to the Jewish hope, as the framework of the Good News.

The faith of Israel, wrought out in the course of centuries of hard experience, was unique among other things in its hope for man's future, both in this age and beyond it. This hope was not escapist or "compensatory." It was grounded in costly experience and it never could have arisen and survived apart from Israel's central concern with righteousness in man and God. Moreover, God's coming salvation was inseparable from his work in the past. Only God the Creator could be God the Renewer or Restorer. In the period that preceded the rise of Christianity, Israel's hope in God was put to extreme tests. We see the emergence of new aspects of the old hope. The expectations of prophet and psalmist had pointed forward to a new age of righteousness and peace on earth. Subsequent writers tended to glorify this new age and to heighten the dramatic features of its inauguration. Here, in the language of the scholar, the older "eschatology" (or doctrine of the end) becomes transcendental. In the apocalypses produced in this period we find various portrayals of the catastrophic features of the end-time, and sublimated portrayals of the Good Time coming. Thus faith evolved new perspectives and new media of expression to convey its confidence in God's coming deliverance and in his resources for dealing with whatever might obstruct his purpose whether in heaven or on earth. This was the matrix of Jesus' message. By using these terms with all their association, Jesus released the thwarted energies of his contemporaries and awoke their deepest memories and loyalties. As Albert Schweitzer has written: "The late-Jewish Messianic world-view is the crater from which burst forth the flame of the eternal religion of love." [1]

Mark begins his account of the active ministry of Jesus with these words:

Now after John was arrested, Jesus came into Galilee, preaching the gospel of God, and saying, "The time is fulfilled, and the kingdom of God is at hand; repent, and believe in the gospel." [1:14, 15]

Here we have stated the theme of Jesus' proclamation throughout his career. His teaching, his healings and exorcisms, the task of the twelve, his whole campaign and even his death, all serve to make good this proclamation and the faith that inspires it. Jesus testifies that in his generation God is bringing in the new age, and this is a matter of good news and of warning. There are other sayings of Jesus which make it clear that Jesus was speaking of the final and definitive end of the old age and of that great world change to which prophets and wise men had looked forward. The early church correctly interpreted the mind of their master in looking forward to the impending judgment and renovation.

It is not our task here to review the evidence in the Gospels for this generally recognized conclusion of modern study. Yet there is almost no point in the New Testament where modern preaching and the views of laymen depart so far from the judgment of scholarship. This is serious since it has to do with the main theme of Jesus' message. It is true that the common

---

[1] *My Life and Thought* (London: Allen & Unwin, 1933), p. 69.

interpretations put upon Jesus' announcement of the kingdom are in part valid. But we should grasp his words in their original sense however difficult this may at first sight appear. We must not modernize the saying, at least not before we understand it as he spoke it.

We can contrast the true import of Jesus' outlook with prevailing misunderstandings as follows. (1) In speaking of the reign of God as "at hand" he was not talking about a mystical kingdom in the soul. When Luke reports Jesus as saying (to the Pharisees!), "the kingdom of God is within you," (A.V.) his words are either mistranslated from the Greek or misreported. Modern scholarship agrees on this. (2) Nor was he announcing a slowly developing movement in history. The parables of the leaven and the mustard seed have been almost universally misinterpreted in this sense in the past, and again modern scholarship must reject the popular view. (3) Nor did Jesus have the church in mind when he spoke of the coming kingdom. Jesus did not announce the church as we understand it or even foresee it. He announced the glorious new age. The only two passages in the Gospels in which he is reported to have mentioned the church are hardly genuine sayings. Even those who like K. L. Schmidt and Cullmann accept the saying, "On this rock I will found my church," give the Greek term here, *ecclesia,* a very special sense derived from the Aramaic word that Jesus may have used. On this view he was not speaking of the "church" as we use the term but of the eschatological community of the new age.

The reign of God as Jesus used the term, and as his hearers understood it, meant the undisputed sovereignty of God over his creation. And this was "at hand." It was coming soon and once-and-for-all. Indeed it was already making its power felt.

It was already present in this sense. (It is true that in another sense the reign of God was a present matter, namely, his universal rule over the world which he had created. For the Jews as for Jesus, God was of old the "great king"—but this aspect of his reign is not at issue in the sayings with which we are here concerned.)

Jesus exulted in the manifest divine action, the new creation in course. God's reign was in process of superseding that of Satan and the demons, so far as they had installed themselves. It was a case of eviction well under way, but affecting heaven and earth. For the disorder was in the whole creation and not only among men. It was a stern matter as well as a gracious one. It was good news and bad news, depending. The point is, "The Lord hasteneth," and men had to come to terms with a love that was impatient, and a purity that could burn, with the zeal of the Lord of hosts.

How could Jesus in all sanity conceive this prodigious expectation and make this kind of cosmic assertion? Let us recall what we have said as to the occasions of such passion and vision as make up an explosive faith. They arise out of extraordinary moral pressures, out of cumulative prayers and frustrations, out of desperate impasses of spiritual need. When the fabric of an old order suffocates men in its debris, their very desperation offers the occasion for a new impulse, a new formula, a new community. This is only suggestive. Of course it is God who speaks to and through such situations, individual or corporate; and in a language, a formula, which men of the time are prepared to recognize.

How then could Jesus entertain such a faith? No doubt in part because it rested on the faith of Israel: Israel's confidence in God the creator, the God of Abraham, Isaac and Jacob, the

God of the Red Sea and of Sinai, the God of deliverances who would also fulfill his promises for the end-time. No doubt also because Jesus saw the signs of the messianic age in his generation. "The time," he said, "is fulfilled." It was now time for the thoughts of many hearts to be revealed. Now at length "the children had come to the birth." The travail of Israel was being accomplished. The pressures and tensions of the time were portentous, whether political and social, or cultural and spiritual. Age-old alternatives, profound and ultimate issues in the life of Israel, and not of Israel alone, all these converged in the consciousness of Jesus and in the public drama of his life. Here was the occasion for God to speak and enact a new thing. This kind of a situation underlies Jesus' proclamation and that proclamation won answering faith from men conditioned by a similar awareness.

II

We propose to inquire now as to why this message had such power. This will serve as a clue to us when we consider its relevance today. For let us make no mistake about it; Jesus' proclamation was like Jeremiah's word of the Lord, like fire, and like the hammer that breaks the rock in pieces. The hearers reported that he spoke as one that had *exousia*—divine power. By his word he shook men's hearts. We can find an analogy for it in Goethe's description of the effects when Napoleon looked at "superfluous persons." "They were pierced through by his glance and saw themselves already shot or beheaded." [2] Jesus' utterance did not always by any means lead men to repentance, but it convulsed them for good or for ill.

---

[2] Quoted by W. M. Dixon, *The Human Situation* (London: E. Arnold, 1937), p. 16.

It is oversimple to say that Jesus' word had power just because it was Jesus who spoke. There is a widespread misunderstanding here as to what the spoken word can accomplish, whether of orator, preacher or even prophet. The audience with its state of mind and heart is always a very large part of it. If it takes two to make a quarrel, it takes two to effect a hearing. There must be the capacity to hear, the "apperception mass." What is necessary where any significant word is grasped is that deep should answer to deep. But the deep in men is not always ready or prepared. The fields are not always white to the harvest. If Jesus' word had power it was not only because it was he that spoke but because Jews of his day were at a point where many could understand if only to deny vehemently.

The message was powerful, in the first place, because Jesus exploited the heights and depths of his people's tradition and memory. He thrust at their deepest experience, capacities and possibilities. He cast a spark into the powder magazine of their deepest will and dream. Just as Jeanne d'Arc knew how to evoke the sleeping possibilities of the French by finding the right formula; just as Hitler could unchain latent energies through an evil divination which told him just what stops to play upon to reach hidden incentives and explosive reservoirs in the life of the German people; so in a greater and truer sense Jesus knew his people and knew how to "find" its soul, to speak to its heart, and to awaken it to responsibility. The point is, however, that to do this Jesus used the leverage of Israel's total world view and world story. That is, he appealed to their understanding of God's way in the world from the beginning of the nation and from the beginning of the world. He proclaimed his message against the background of Jahweh's working in creation, vocation, deliverance, covenant and promise. "The time is fulfilled, and the kingdom of God is at hand" meant, along with his healings, exorcisms, parables, that everything most deeply important to the Jew, however neglected, obscured, buried, was now at stake, brought to light, and on the point of fulfillment. Jesus sought to challenge, evoke, mobilize, crystallize all the latent loyalties in Israel. To do this he invoked their total memory whether historical or "mythical." His message only took on its supreme meaning and crucial character because the whole record of the past was but prologue to it.

We have here, then, a clue to the power of Jesus' message: a message concerning the end, an "eschatological" message, indeed, and for that very reason one that meant a total hope and a total claim. The Christian today, especially the Christian preacher, will give this clue long consideration. How today can we bring a similar leverage to bear upon the men of our time? A theology of history is required as well as an ultimate trust in God, and these must be presented in evocative symbol, that is, in the appropriate rhetoric of faith.

The message was powerful, in the second place, because the situation was in certain respects propitious. We have already touched on this in connection with Jesus' own faith. The fields were "white to the harvest." God was already at work in a new way when Jesus came. The kingdom brought Jesus in as true a sense as Jesus brought the kingdom. "The thoughts of many hearts" were ready to be revealed. There were those waiting in heightened expectancy for the consolation of Israel; the consolation of Israel, that is, in the purest sense. They waited for God's righteousness to be revealed, however it might affect Israel's then institutions. It was felt that the world

was growing old. It was time for the great annunciation. Yes.
both among Jews and Greeks. The world of that time had its
groups and strata that were like a whispering gallery ready to
give back the cry. In Israel this was not like Isaiah's situation
when the challenged watchman replies that there is no news:

> The morning cometh, and also the night:
> if ye will inquire, inquire ye: return, come. [21:12]

It was a situation, rather, where the Lord's watchman, aware
that the greater day has dawned, cries out to the city:

> Arise, shine; for thy light is come,
> And the glory of the Lord is risen upon thee.
> For, behold, the darkness shall cover the earth,
> And gross darkness the people:
> But the Lord shall arise upon thee,
> And his glory shall be seen upon thee.
> And the Gentiles shall come to thy light,
> And kings to the brightness of thy rising. [Is. 60:1–3]

We need to remind ourselves of the ecstatically sublime poetry
of Isaiah, the Psalms and the Canticles of Luke if we are to
appreciate the true character of the expectation and elation of
those circles in which the Gospel arose. This was the kind of
tinder which the spark of the good news ignited.

There was a preparation for the Gospel in certain circles in
Israel in the sense that all its experience past and present—
both with outside nations and with inner tensions—had
brought it to a phase of maturity, an hour of parturition. This
crisis showed itself in ways that ranged from febrile "political"
manifestations to ambiguous psychological and cultural symp-
toms. Humanly speaking, this juncture, which had almost the
character of a paroxysm and which betrayed itself in various
forms of hysteria, gave birth to Christianity and not long after

to a reconstruction of Judaism. The emergence of John the Baptist, this long-postponed renewal of prophecy in Israel, testifies to the deeper drama and to the revolution that was imminent.[3]

III

So far we have been looking back to the first century in an attempt to identify Jesus' message in his own setting and to account for its relevance and power in that day. Many of the terms he used such as Satan, judgment, Son of Man, we have not examined in particular, but we have given attention to his use of the Jewish world picture and especially the idea of the reign of God.

Let us turn, then, to the question of how far and in what way Jesus' proclamation of the kingdom is relevant today. To be quite honest about it, this proclamation in the words and with the sense he employed is not easily available to us. We must give full recognition to the difficulty here. No doubt we can modernize the Good News and even with much warrant. We can say that the kingdom is within us; and there is a certain truth in this. Or we can assure men that the day of justice and peace on earth is slowly dawning; and this author for one will agree that this is a legitimate modernization of part of Jesus' faith. But these views and others (adventist or Barthian or ecclesiastical interpretations of the kingdom) do not take Jesus' expectation at its face value, nor do they do full justice to it. There is no getting around it, we must recog-

[3] "Especially in the apocalyptic circles of Judaism is the tension great. The consciousness that 'the world hasteth fast to pass away' (II Esdras 4:26) is dominant. This kind of hope stirs especially the 'quiet in the land' in their oppressed economic relationships." Herbert Preisker, *Geist und Leben: Das Telos-Ethos Der Urchristentum* (Guttersloh, 1923), p. 11.

F

nize the strangeness of his outlook (as well as the gigantic character of his underlying faith, which is perhaps our greatest
difficulty), and then engage in a radical task of reformulation.
Indeed, it may be that we shall not be able to find modern
terms at all points into which we can translate his message.
In any case we cannot today take his words on our lips in the
sense he gave them. We cannot announce the impending advent of the Son of Man on the clouds and a forensic world
judgment of a final character, nor can we say that God's reign
is today in its final stage of ending all evil here and now. Nor
can many today be altogether happy with an interpretation of
evil in terms of Satan and demonic agency.

At this point it becomes necessary to say something about
the conceptions of this kind which Jesus and his contemporaries used in their portrayal of history and judgment and evil.
In our foregoing chapter we have spoken of the special character of the language of faith. Spiritual things have to be expressed in spiritual language. Faith has to use mythopoetic
terms. It is true that such terms are often also related to obsolete ways of understanding history and nature. But this last
limitation is not so serious. We all recognize that great literature and art often evidence the transient and parochial conceptions of their day, and this does not prevent us from laying
hold of what is great and permanent in them. What concerns
us rather in the case of Jesus' language about the kingdom is
how far he spoke, as we say, "literally," and how far "symbolically." If we suggest that Jesus spoke symbolically or
imaginatively about the judgment and the new age, we do not
mean that he spoke fancifully or in fictions. He was talking
about real things and a real future. But neither was he speaking literally, prosaically or woodenly. This is a false alterna-

tive. In this area the Jewish and early Christian language of faith and expectancy was neither literal nor consciously symbolic, but in its proper sense, naïve. Intimations of human destiny in the light of experience were expressed in the only terms in which such realities could then be formulated.

We have also to come to terms with the fact that Jesus proclaimed the judgment and the new age as near at hand. This need not disturb us as it did those for whom Johannes Weiss and Albert Schweitzer first clearly raised the problem. We can learn something from the suggestion that Jesus "saw eternity in an hour," that he "foreshortened history," that he transferred his sense of the nearness of God from the spiritual to the temporal order, that a new creation did in a sense begin with his work, and that he used the parables of faith to convey the destiny of the world and of man. Such considerations should help us to understand Jesus' proclamation of the kingdom as well as its nearness, and thus prepare us to deal more wisely with the question of its relevance for us.

We have frankly recognized that there is much in Jesus' proclamation that is alien to our thinking and not available to us today in its original form. We now approach the crux of our discussion. For we are convinced that rightly understood his message has still indispensable relevance and truth. We are faced here with a double task. We want to know what this continuing truth is. And we want to be able to declare it with its proper dynamic for our time.

To find the abiding truth in Jesus' message some would say that we have only to strip off the husk of prescientific conceptions, remove the contemporary errors: the eschatology, the demonology, the naïve anthropomorphism. Then we shall have the timeless truths that we can preach today, whether the

fatherhood of God and brotherhood of man, or Jesus' ex-
emplification of moral will and reverence for life. But any such
procedure leads to a mutilation of Jesus' outlook. The fatherhood of God is good Judaism, the brotherhood of man is good
Stoicism, reverence for life is good Buddhism. All of these no
doubt are also good Christianity, but to stop with these or
other similar articles of faith, say the kingdom of God on earth
or the immortality of the soul, is to miss a great deal of what
Jesus meant. To make a distinction between husk and kernel
or between outer form and inner substance is always a misleading method in dealing with the truth of the past. The
greater a religious message or writing is, the more indissoluble
is its form and substance. This makes our task of restating the
truth of the past more difficult, but it means that we are less
likely to mutilate the truth and to throw away what is essential
with what seems unessential.

There are some interpreters of Jesus' message of the kingdom who do not make this mistake. They take his dramatic
expectation seriously but they allegorize it and make it into a
parable of grace and judgment *here and now* for any man or
any generation that hears it. The kingdom, then, does not
really refer to a future reality but a present one. The last judgment and the new creation are offered to us at every moment
of decision, especially in every hour of crisis, or in every service
of worship. This view can be referred back to Kierkegaard,
and comes to expression in some exponents of what is called
"realized eschatology." What this view forfeits is the future
hope for man implicit in Jesus' message. Oscar Cullmann has
shown how untrue these versions are to the real time sense and
hope of early Christianity.[4]

[4] *Christ and Time.*

Other ways of dealing with Jesus' outlook can be mentioned. Some, on the one hand, still look forward to a literal fulfillment of his words in a coming of the Son of Man with the clouds to judgment. Some, on the other hand, disallow his apocalyptic language and define the kingdom as a perfected social order. So the pendulum swings between highly otherworldly interpretations of his meaning and social-Utopian ones. We would not wish to leave an impression, however, that scholarly interpretation today is hopelessly divergent. We have learned to take Jesus' language about the consummation seriously and have come to recognize the sublime hope it conveys. Our chief remaining difficulty concerns its seeming otherworldliness, and it is with this misunderstanding that we must especially concern ourselves.

IV

If now we pay due regard to the imaginative language Jesus used and the tradition in which he used it, we may venture to modernize his words and say that he was announcing a sublime Tomorrow for mankind, or rather for that remnant of mankind that would fulfill the conditions required. This sublime Tomorrow was already dawning for his generation—not just a new epoch but a new creation—and its signs were already manifest. This new Tomorrow would necessarily come in with the universal throes of the struggle of light with darkness; with thunder and lightning, hail and tempest, "as the dawn comes in the Pyrenees." To change the figure, the present age would pass into the new age only through the gates of birth.[5]

---

[5] II Esdras 7:3–14 presents this theme of the narrow gate under various figures.

But, it will be objected, this idea of a sublime Tomorrow is vague. Did not the Jewish hope speak more definitely? Did not Jesus, indeed, announce the end of this age, the coming of the Son of Man with the clouds, the last judgment, the separation of the good and the evil, the coming of a heavenly kingdom? At the Last Supper did he not assure his disciples that after his death he would be reunited with them in the coming kingdom? It is true that Jesus used such language. On the one hand, however, we should not literalize and harden the terms he used. This whole complex of symbols needs to be understood in the light of Old Testament antecedents. Professor Paul Minear has well shown in connection with such details of the judgment as the clouds of heaven, the earthquake motif, the last trumpet, how wrong it is to take these in a crassly literal fashion.[6] Their significance lies in their associations.

Furthermore, we may well distinguish between various stages of formulation of this material as we find it in the Gospels. The evangelists have certainly gone beyond Jesus himself in their elaboration of coming events. Borrowing from the existing Jewish portrayal of the end-time, they have often made explicit what was left implicit by him. In doing so they did not necessarily betray his outlook. But their additions do tend to disguise the sovereign freedom with which he used the great images of judgment and renewal.

Thus Jesus did assuredly speak of the immediate coming of the heavenly Son of Man-Judge to usher in the new age, but he does not speak of the end of the "world." It is the Gospels which fill in the picture with their details of the Great Assize and the adjudication of final rewards and penalties. Jesus

[6] Paul Minear, *Christian Hope and the Second Coming* (Philadelphia: Westminster, 1854), Pt. II.

himself speaks of God's prompt vindication of those who cry to him out of oppression, but it is the church which amplifies his words with accounts of the penal action of the angels. It is Jesus who encourages his followers with the prospect of the messianic banquet in the new age, but it is the author of the Fourth Gospel and not Jesus who says, "My kingdom is not of this world." Though Jesus says in the Beatitudes, "Great is your reward in heaven" this does not mean that his followers will "go to heaven when they die." It means that they have reward stored up before God, that they have "treasure in heaven." This reward will be enjoyed not "in heaven" but in the new age, in the kingdom of God, which is not the same thing as heaven.

No doubt the sublime hope of the Jews and of Jesus anticipated a wonderful new age to which the righteous dead would arise, but this did not mean the "end of the world" or dissolution of the creation, but rather the transformation of the creation. Sometimes, indeed, in later Jewish and Christian writings the idealization of the future did assert the end of this world and a wholly new creation, but in such cases we can recognize the hyperbole of the poet. The fact is that the Jewish outlook shared by Jesus did not distinguish sharply between an earthly future and a transcendent future. The two were commonly merged. Otherworldly language was used to portray the splendors of the new age but a timeless angelic and purely spiritual existence was not intended. Apocalyptic symbols could be used to represent what we call earthly events.[7]

[7] In the seventh chapter of Daniel we have a very important example of this, since the later imagery of the coming of the Son of Man with the clouds of heaven as the initial event of the New Age has here a direct antecedent. The vision of Daniel in this chapter discloses in apocalyptic symbolism the course of events on earth. Four beasts are represented as successively ruling on earth, actually representing the great world powers

This kind of argument can be pressed further. It can be shown that Jesus used parables of the new age, such as that of the new temple which would replace the one to be destroyed, which were far from suggesting a sheerly supernatural future.

But there is a better approach than this to the supposed otherworldly character of Jesus' eschatology. Our error consists in the assumptions with which we come to it. We pose questions to him which are out of order. Thanks to the crisis of his time and calling, Jesus was speaking out of a depth where man is made and unmade, where the world and the future were molten and plastic. He gave voice to the unpredictable possibilities of mankind in the hands of God. We take too much for granted the accustomed limits and co-ordinates of our own experience. We underestimate the dynamics of life and their appropriate expression. We do not do justice to great faith and its peculiar language. To Jesus standing at those spiritual frontiers, at those portals giving on human destiny, it could not occur to make *this* prediction with regard to time and *that* with regard to eternity. And what is of cardinal importance to us is that he spoke with regard to ultimates. There was time enough later for the church to conclude as to the implications for this age or for that age, and to adapt itself to the delay of the end. Because the church itself shared the elemental faith and passion of Christ, this adaptation was not a crucial problem.[8]

Babylon, the Medes, Persia, Greece. But then came before the Ancient of Days "one like unto a Son of Man" to whom was given dominion and power, and we are told that he stands for "the saints of the Most High," i.e., for Israel. The celestial symbols represent a transfer of power from the nations to Israel.

[8] When deep faith was lacking, Christians gave too much attention to the matter of just when the kingdom would come. The New Testament has to teach some that it is "later than they think" and others that it is not as late as they think. See also Minear, *Eyes of Faith* (Philadelphia: Westminster, 1946), pp. 233–35.

In his situation Jesus became the voice of Israel's ancient and inspired hopes, forecasting a sublime Tomorrow, "in stupor at the uncharted things to come" (Dante). To convey something of the august character of this future he naturally availed himself of whatever symbolism was available whether the transcendental variety or the more sober kind. Sometimes he characterized the new age in terms of the resurrection life, sometimes in traditional imagery of a more mundane kind: thrones or tables.

But the point we are driving toward is that the transcendental imagery which Jesus used in this context must not be misinterpreted as evidence of otherworldliness on his part. It does not represent escapism. It is an affirmation of life, here and hereafter, both. No pagan or Renaissance or Romantic affirmation of life has ever approached it in power or elation. Of course Jesus' augury of blessedness was selective. It was not all life, all culture that was affirmed, though Jesus could see possibilities in unlikely circles.

Thus in seeking the relevance of Jesus' proclamation that the kingdom of God was immediately at hand, we have to go behind the language of his faith and seek to feel the force of that faith itself. The church through the decades and centuries has sought to do this, changing the white light of his ultimate vision into a spectrum of particular implications.

We can find confirmation in the later history of the church of the observations we have made with regard to the sublime goals set forth in the New Testament. The idea of the kingdom of God or the kingdom of heaven never becomes irrelevant to men's life on earth as long as the church holds its great faith in potent form. It is only vitiated and sterile phases of the Christian life which fix their attention upon the "pie in the sky"; it is only secondhand and wooden versions of the faith which are consistently dualistic, otherworldly and pessimistic. The Gospel can, however, exhibit its inherent relation to the life of this world in different ways.

Illustrations of these variants can be found in connection with the Great Awakening as described by Professor Richard Niebuhr in his book, *The Kingdom of God in America*.[9] As a background we may recall that many of the founders of New England, like their Puritan contemporaries in the England of the time of Cromwell, anticipated the fulfillment of God's promises to his people and the world after no long delay.

> At the end of the period of settlement the tension of men toward the coming Kingdom slackened. As the sovereignty of God became the rule of an absentee monarch . . . so the coming kingdom, insofar as it was judgment, became a familiar and unreal crisis; insofar as it was promise it came to be either a fairly certain future prosperity and peace or an equally comfortable heaven. . . .
> The Great Awakening and the revivals were ushered in by a new awareness of the coming kingdom. Edwards and Wesley, like Paul and Luther before them, became intensely conscious of the great gap which exists between human performance and divine demand or between the actuality and potentiality of human life. . . . The idea of the coming kingdom came alive when it was connected with the conviction of God's living power.[10]

But Professor Niebuhr then goes on to show how the power of the experience led to a shift of interest "from the eternal Kingdom into which souls enter one by one to the kingdom coming upon earth." Leaders of various types, Edwards, Hopkins, Wesley, Woolman, shared in a this-worldly hope which was safeguarded from utopianism as long as the primary

[9] New York: Harper, 1937.
[10] *Ibid.*, pp. 135–37.

vision of the kingdom was maintained in its purity. The later romantic or rationalist versions of the American dream have preserved something of the true religious sanctions. The secular optimism that has adulterated them is in course of purification by hard experience, and the underlying Christian hope for society is then better recognized.

Only a complete misunderstanding of Jesus' outlook can ascribe to him an otherworldly asceticism or an indifference to man's actual life in this world. That he should have dealt austerely with men and spoken of the gaining and losing of life cannot be charged to otherworldliness. Nor can his use of the current images for rewards and punishments be so charged since these were the least significant of the motives for ethics found in either Judaism or his own teaching. It is, indeed, true that Jesus dealt with the needs of men at a deeper level than that with which modern humanitarianism is rightly much concerned. Yet such issues as those we associate with economic security and social values were implicitly involved in his work and teaching.

Primitive Christianity was not motivated by compensatory dreams of satisfactions in the world to come, though the hope of these satisfactions was secure.[11] When the church was true to itself it was not motivated by eudemonistic rewards in another life as wages for an exploited proletariat which found life in the Roman Empire intolerable without illusions! These perverse and plausible half-truths of Nietzsche and the Marxists and Sir James Frazer represent the most deadly and dangerous libel on Christianity that the modern world has produced. If

[11] The substance of this paragraph and the next are taken from the author's *Eschatology and Ethics in the Teachings of Jesus*, rev. ed. (London: S.C.M. Press, 1950), pp. 69–70.

there is one confusion more than any other which is responsible for the apostasy from Christianity of intellectuals and
those they have influenced everywhere in the Western world
and in communist lands, it has to do with this charge of otherworldliness and asceticism. Indeed, it involves a whole group
of confusions: Jewish Messianism was the compensatory vision
of a frustrated people; Jesus was a naïve dreamer conditioned
by a simple society or a deluded fanatic; his ethics was an impracticable perfectionism and the early church's version of it
a slave morality which offered a sentimental and ascetic code
in exchange for that heroism from which they were disqualified by their social position. Even Christian moralists and
theologians have difficulty in coming to terms with these issues.
There is no area which demands more attention today in
Christian apologetics, and biblical scholarship and interpretation are crucial at this point.

What we have to insist, then, is that Jesus' proclamation of
the kingdom was not a fantasy projection nor the portrayal of
an escapist's paradise. It was a prophetic forecast of human
destiny resting on the whole of Israel's best experience, and
her witness to the agelong purpose and work of God the Creator. This forecast had to do with ultimates and it rested on
ultimates. It had to do with last things and it rested on first
things. But it was directed to the present moment and was
lived out in the concrete process of history, and it bore on that
concrete process in its present and future aspects. The emancipation which Jesus announced as good news to the multitudes
was something far more actual than a promise of spiritual
rewards in a world to come.

To carry over or transplant the substance of Jesus' message
into the present day means that we must combine his august

hope for man with some such setting as he gave it in his people's witness to the living God. The hope must spring out of and be relevant to all of man's deepest tragedy and bondage. The eternal aspects of his hope are not enough by themselves, though they are a part of it. The this-worldly implications of his hope are to be insisted on, though they too are not the whole story. So far as our world picture and our world consciousness have changed we must annotate and clarify Jesus' Good News of the sublime Tomorrow which is already dawning. But that Good News will lose its force unless we retain its context and guarantees in ultimates in God himself.

Any adequate modernizing of the Good News, moreover, must use the language of faith; it must be couched in imaginative and emotionally charged symbols, even as it is borne up upon a tide of ardor and passion. We must find and exploit the sacred poetry and story, the evocative imagery, art and parable that will ignite the smoldering aspirations and moral energies of our Western peoples. Our great resource here is the Scripture. Its material is still alive for us not only in the Bible itself but in the hymn book, in Christian art and music, in cantatas and spirituals, in literature and common speech, and in our great observances of Christmas, Good Friday and Easter, not to mention our commoner observances of prayer, preaching and sacrament. All such symbolism, when it is properly animated and when it is sensitively approached, has the power to introduce us in some degree into that level of experience of which we have spoken in connection with Jesus where man is made and unmade, where the world is shaped and reshaped, where the bondage of necessity or social and psychological patterns is dissolved.

To alter fate is God's prerogative.[12]

But non-Christian and semi-Christian cultures have their own intimations of faith, and symbols and vehicles for them, and daily life throws up its contemporary analogies. The general aspirations of men, speaking in romantic or idealistic terms, need to be corrected, but when they spring from profound need and devotion they bear something of the same relation to the Christian hope as the messianic prophecies of the old covenant. Sad experience has taught and will teach the romantic and the utopian that their hope must not rest in man's creative vitalities alone, nor in social orderings and technology. But Thoreau's

> The earth is but a morning star,

and Vachel Lindsay's

> They spoke, I think, of perils past,
> They spoke, I think, of peace at last.
> One thing I remember:
> Spring came on forever
> Spring came on forever. . . .[13]

and Carlyle's assertion that the constellations are only porch lights of the greater glory to which man is destined: These are moving and unreprovable analogies of the Christian hope.

A viewpoint like this with regard to the eschatology of Jesus makes it possible once more to take up his "parables of the kingdom" and find new meaning in them. Modern study has made it clear that the parable of the leaven does not refer to a slow growth of the kingdom in society, nor does the parable of the mustard seed. Both call attention to the unostentatious

---

[12] *The Sonnets of Michel Angelo Buonarroti* (London: John Murray, 1912), p. 80.

[13] "The Chinese Nightingale," *Collected Poems* by Vachel Lindsay, p. 34. Copyright, 1917, 1945, by The Macmillan Company. Used by permission.

character of the kingdom in its beginnings, and both draw attention to the amazing disproportion between the initial stages and the outcome. The "when" is not under consideration, nor the "how" of the process save so far as God himself is the agent. So also with Mark's parable of the earth bearing fruit of itself; "first the blade, then the ear, then the full grain in the ear." But if Jesus is speaking of the coming of the kingdom from a level which is not concerned with what we call "history" but only with God's future and with human destiny generally, then these parables come into their own. They convey an intimation of the ineffable outcomes of life. They translate the apocalyptic eschatological symbol into lowly and popular images drawn from daily toil. The instinct of Christian piety has often so understood these parables though modern social idealism has limited their import in one way and pietism in another (often wrongly giving them an individual application).

But if we recognize that Jesus in these parables is affirming the new creation under way and the connection of the unimaginable goals of life with his humble work—in a supreme vision passing over our distinction of "history" versus eternity—we then have the right to modernize and to apply this expectation to history, provided we abide by his standpoint and his criteria. A degree of fulfillment of God's work in history and society is a proper application of his outlook. The sublime Tomorrow which he forecast includes this hope too, though we must be as serious with his theme of judgment as with his theme of promise.

V

There are many Christians today who repudiate the hope of human betterment. Among these are numbered especially many leaders in Europe who have proven their devotion to the Gospel under persecution. Not only is any idea of automatic progress rightly rejected, but even any expectation of substantial and enduring gains in human well-being. It is recognized that conditions here or there, in one generation or another, may make possible dazzling achievements in the arts or technology, or even momentary periods of social achievement. But as long as man is the finite creature he is and has the make-up with which the past has endowed him ("it is known what man is"), there can be no real advance. To Christians who think this way the story of man's emergence from savagery is no counter argument. The more civilized he becomes the more disastrous are his appetites and conflicts. Every civilization, it is said, is only one generation removed from barbarism! The conclusion then is that any assured human felicity such as is announced in the messianic hopes of the Old Testament must be assigned to a new creation or to life beyond death. Bible students find confirmation for such pessimism in their interpretation of writings like the Apocalypse. Jesus' proclamation of the kingdom and its dramatic advent is conformed to the same pattern of otherworldliness. A final silencer may be applied to those who demur by invoking what science tells us of the inevitable final disaster to life on our planet.

Such views would seem to reckon too lightly both with the story of human culture and with the power of the Holy Spirit. There is wisdom for us in these matters in the findings of anthropology and evolution as well as in Scripture. It is anomalous that the theologian should find himself in the company of the cynic in holding that there is no progress in matters that count. Common sense and competent cultural study appear to disagree. Theology is too often blinded at this point by some defensive dogma: it begrudges (like Jonah) any divine charities in the human story outside the rigid channels it would demarcate. Or theology overstates its timely warning against utopianism. Or theology is unduly swayed by contemporary tragedies. But the disasters of today should lead the theologian to confession of the sins of his church and his nation rather than to a general cultural pessimism.

One can apply to those who disbelieve in the improvement of mankind the words of Jesus: "You know neither the scriptures nor the power of God" [Mk. 12:24]. By the Scriptures here we mean, first of all, the messianic hopes of the Old Testament. These hopes were not otherworldly but mundane. The message of Jesus involves no contradiction of this mundane promise but rather a deepening and transfiguring of it. The biblical-theological mood of today really makes the New Testament contradict the Old on this major point. It should be recognized that the late Jewish and early Christian modification of the earlier messianism adds the resurrection hope and the eternal hope without canceling the social hope.

But the chief charge today against those who surrender hope for mankind is that they limit the power of God. To narrow the effective redemptive work of the Spirit to the life beyond the grave reflects an impoverishment of Christian faith, hope and love, and plays into the hands of those who scorn the Gospel as an opiate of the people.

The Christian who rightly labors for the banishment of evil from the earth must, however, dissociate himself from shallow versions of this hope. The greater goals of faith are truly beyond our life in the flesh though not discontinuous with it.[14] That social humanitarianism, whether Christian or secular, which flatters itself on its this-worldliness and waives the life

[14] Cf. "The New Society in the New Age" (III, E), in *The Biblical Doctrine of Man in Society*, G. Ernest Wright (London: S. C. M. Press, 1954).

beyond, knows all too little of the human heart. More abundant life on earth will only come as a by-product or even as a footnote to a transcendent dimension of faith and hope.

A Christian view of "progress" is peculiar, moreover, in its emphasis on the doctrine of the remnant. If there is one clear lesson taught both by evolution and the prophets it is that of the discarding of the great majorities, the winnowing out of species and nations and classes. As in the past, so in the future, the powers that be will often go into the discard. But to recognize this is not to agree with the biblical realists who say that there can be no considerable actualization upon earth of the kingdom of God. "When thy judgments are in the earth the inhabitants of the world learn righteousness" (Is. 26:9). A Christian hope for mankind stands or falls with the action of the living God and must be prepared to reckon with his severity. As in the case of the individual, the processes of discipline and disaster are but the disguises of his beneficent purpose. The Christian preacher will therefore not say Peace, Peace, when there is no peace. But to the meek and the penitent, to the responsible and the compassionate, he will announce the time when wars shall be no more and peace shall come down like rain upon the mown grass.

The Christian rests his hope for a better world on the work of the Spirit in the church, on the leavening influence of the faithful in the life of the world, on the self-destruction of rival ways of life, the self-elimination of false ideologies in a world to which they are inadequate, and on the irresistible extension of the Christian faith to all portions of humanity. Reversions of parts of Christendom to godlessness or idolatrous cults of nationalism only succeed in highlighting the inadequacy of such ways of life. But it is only as the Christian lives his faith that error comes to recognize itself. A significant hope for mankind can be sustained only where the renewing power of the faith has free course. "I, when I am lifted up from the earth, will draw all men to myself." It is in vain that the world will look elsewhere for its true health.

But how, it will be said, can we reconcile such a hope for some real fulfillment of the kingdom of God on earth with what science has to tell us of the doom of the whole human race on a dying planet? Our solar system, we are told, is temporary and our earth, once uninhabitable, will sometime be uninhabitable again. Evidently this reminds us that all temporal hopes have their limits. Our present creaturely life already has its analogous limitations in natural catastrophes, in disease and death. Just as mankind has learned to mitigate some of these fatalities and put an end to others, so we can expect it to do the same in far greater measure. Thus a new glacial age need not be a threat to the race in the future. The final extinction of man through "natural causes" may be viewed as too remote to constitute a practical problem, though we have here certainly a theological problem. There are those who argue that the future of nature must always remain an open question since we have to do with the living God and his freedom. Such thinking is highly speculative. We must recognize the limits of historical existence both for the individual and the race. Even so the inevitability of death for the individual does not or should not lead us to slight the maximum possible fulfillment of his temporal life. So the inevitability of the death of the race should not discourage us from seeking the maximum attainment of human well-being and culture in the interim.

In insisting that the august hope of the kingdom of God as

Jesus voiced it has its bearing on human progress, we do not overlook the terrible potentialities for destruction of modern methods of warfare. We have here only an accentuation in the present era of history of a perennial aspect of human insecurity. We have not maintained that human society would move toward greater unity and well-being without convulsions and catastrophes. It is the remnant that carries the legacy of the past, the purposes of God and the hope of the future. The time comes when the endowment of the remnant diffuses itself through the peoples to a degree which inhibits the greater conflicts. In the present era as in the past, what is crucial is not the presence or absence of particular engines of destruction but the motives of their provision or use. "He that taketh the sword shall perish by the sword." Applied to the factors of power in the modern world, this law does not condemn the arms themselves but their irresponsible use. Our hope in such a situation lies in the assurance that evil eliminates itself. The warning holds for ourselves as well as for others. Nevertheless, throughout whatever disasters and retributions a remnant will remain. The meek shall inherit the earth—and these are by no means necessarily the disarmed.[15]

These kinds of mundane auguries and speculations will no

15   A thought is with me sometimes, and I say—
        Should the whole frame of earth by inward throes
        Be wrenched, or fire come down from far to scorch
        Her pleasant habitations, and dry up
        Old Ocean, in his bed left singed and bare,
        Yet would the living Presence still subsist
        Victorious, and composure would ensue,
        And kindlings like the morning—presage sure
        Of day returning and of life revived.

Wordsworth, *The Excursion,* I, lines 927–30. Cited by Willard L. Sperry in connection with the Wordsworth Centennial at Princeton University.

doubt appear fleshly-minded and frivolous to many Christians today who have felt the validity and depth of neo-orthodox witness. The two emphases do not rule each other out. On the other hand, many statements we read today about the Christian hope betray such a jealous and febrile vigilance against admitting any kind or degree of earthly improvement that we are tempted to call in the psychologist as we would with a neurotic parent who smothers every impulse to self-expression and spontaneity on the part of his own child. One feels that a morbidity lurks here connected with the constantly reiterated themes of guilt and forgiveness, pride and retribution, slavery and freedom. These are indeed evangelical themes but they can be turned to highly otherworldly if not masochistic purposes.

VI

The doctrine of the second coming of Christ is a problem for the modern mind which inevitably presents itself in the present connection. How do we fit the return of Christ and the last judgment into our understanding of the future? Jesus' proclamation of the kingdom did not include an announcement of his second advent in the form in which the Gospels and the New Testament teach it. He did announce the immediate coming of the Son of Man as God's agent of final judgment and renewal. Jesus was not as specific about the circumstances of the judgment as the Gospels make him out to be. He no doubt varied in his representation of the final climax just as the Jews of his time did. Sometimes they saw God himself and alone as the judge. Sometimes a dramatic judgment scene was pictured such as is ascribed to Jesus in Matt. 25:31–46. Sometimes it was sufficient to picture the gathering out of the righteous to their blessed reward. This fluidity of conception in the Jewish-Christian mythology of the end-time is a commonplace of historical study. It should warn us against too literal a reading of the portrayals we find. If we take these pictures literally we do more than the Jews and early Christians did. What was important to them will, however, still be important to us: days of reckoning if not a day of reckoning, and God's governance of men and nations to the end of the story.

If Jesus did not himself claim to be the divine agent at the judgment, at least he presented discipleship to his own person as the test of approval at the coming of the Son of Man.

For whoever is ashamed of me and of my words in this adulterous and sinful generation, of him will the Son of man also be ashamed, when he comes in the glory of his Father with the holy angels. [Mark 8:38; cf. Luke 12:8–9]

The church in the light of his resurrection inevitably identified Jesus with the Son of Man who was to come, as is evident in the way this very passage is understood in its context in Mark. Thus it proclaimed his future return in glory. Jesus had been content to promise his reunion with his chosen in the life of the new age. His followers elaborated the drama of his second coming as the counterpart to the tremendous symbolism with which they invested his resurrection and ascension. Shattering events and experiences properly called forth stupendous and paradoxical expression, borrowing and reshaping the available imagery of the time.

We must recognize the problem presented for modern readers of the Scripture by this aspect of the teaching. The time is past when such features of the New Testament could be skirted out of deference to cherished pieties. There are too many today for whom such doctrines are occasions of stumbling if not scandal. We must frankly concede that no such dramatic return of Christ with the clouds is to be expected in the course of history. He has his own way of coming but not this way.

Indeed theologians today in speaking of the parousia do not themselves understand it in literal fashion. Yet they reiterate the biblical language concerning the parousia and the last judgment as though the terms were self-explanatory. One instance of this has been the successive reports of the Advisory Commission of the World Council of Churches, dealing with the Christian hope. The third and final report is in many respects a notable and in parts a magnificent testimony, and one which powerfully relates the Christian hope both to various false hopes and to particular aspects of the Christian life. One section of it effectively proclaims a considerable scope for constructive social activity in the present age and thus a real measure of this-worldly hope. It is here rightly insisted that Christian social action in history bears abiding fruits. Finally, it is made clear that the history of the world will not be swept aside as irrelevant or meaningless at the consummation. Real effort is made to interpret the imagery of judgment and the return of Christ, particularly by the characterization of Christ as the "boundary" of all of life. Yet this task is not radically undertaken. It was no doubt thought of as leading too far afield, as was stated at one point in the discussion of the Commission. Many members of the Commission represented churches whose members find no difficulty in the traditional biblical images. Yet in presenting the Christian understanding of hope to the world these interpreters should have had in mind the vast multitudes of modern men including many believers for whom these canonized formulas constitute stumbling blocks.

Clarification of this matter should begin with a double recognition: (1) that the New Testament doctrine of the return of Christ (or Jesus' announcement of the coming of the Son of Man) belongs to the order of symbolic and mythopoetic statement and was not understood literally in the late Jewish and early Christian religion; and (2) that (as Professor Paul Minear has so well shown in his volume, *The Christian Hope and the Second Coming*) a just understanding of the teaching is only possible in the light of the whole complex or pattern of biblical experience. To grasp, for example, what the coming of the Messiah *with the clouds* meant, we must recall what the "clouds of heaven" meant as associated with the action of God in Israel's faith. The first Christians with their vivid sense of the divine challenge to Israel and the nations spoke in the language available to them of what could neither be doubted nor delayed: the assertion of God's control over history. And they knew that this action of the Lord of history would turn upon the figure of the Christ and would involve the vindication of his first coming.

What we call history takes on a special character in the light of the Bible. We learn there that it is not just a boundless panorama of episodes, an anarchy of waves and cross-currents, as it must appear to the man who surveys the innumerable tribes and peoples of all parts of the world and who thinks in terms of the millennia. The Bible's conspectus of creation, redemption and last judgment, while it recognizes the multitudes of peoples and kindreds, sees history in terms of a plot. Every part and every time stand in relation to the plot. There is meaning, providence, relatedness, discipline throughout, even down to the most obscure events and persons. It is true that the New Testament picture of the last judgment took shape in a world the dimensions of whose measurement of space and time were diminutive as compared with ours. Yet this symbol may still dramatize for us the truth that all history makes up one pattern, hidden though it may be to our observation. It also suggests that all history prepares a harvest, moves toward a consummation—likewise hidden to our assessment—which will sum up all that has gone before. And the New Testament finds the secret or law of this pervasive pattern in Christ, in terms of whom also its manifestation will appear.

To return to our main theme: we can count upon the ultimate assent of many to the message of Good News, for there is that in the human heart that cries out for fulfillment. Illustrations from the poets could be multiplied.

Browning, "A Death in the Desert":

Man partly is and wholly hopes to be. . . .

Browning, *Paracelsus:*

. . . so in man's self arise
August anticipations, symbols, types
Of a dim splendour ever on before. . . .

That the hope is not a romantic optimism but based on purgation needs to be remembered, however, and of this aspect we are reminded in T. S. Eliot's "Little Gidding":

And all shall be well and
All manner of thing shall be well
By the purification of the motive
In the ground of our beseeching.[16]

Men have intimations not only of immortality but of a sublime Tomorrow on earth, as the messianic movement in the

[16] *Four Quartets* (London: Faber & Faber Ltd., 1943), p. 37. Used by permission of the publishers.

Old Testament teaches. All that the race has known in the past of disaster and tribulation and heartbreak must only be prologue. To this craving the words of Jesus make answer: The kingdom of God is at hand—ever at hand, and in a degree ever within reach. Our Christian good news will affirm the same hope—taking account indeed of all the miscarriages and forfeits of time, past, present and future—but resting its hopes upon the deepest foundations and assigning the remedy to these evils to the ultimate source.

We shall affirm that the sublime Tomorrow has reference both to this world and to the life beyond. Man is a creature that is born to be surpassed. We know not what we shall be. Here we are, as Dante says, but *entomata in diffeto,* larvae that fall short of their true nature. "The earnest expectation of the creature waiteth for the manifestation of the sons of God." The promise in all such auguries must not be restricted to the life to come.

IV

the message of paul

The righteousness of God is revealed. . . .
ROMANS 1:17

Behold therefore the goodness and severity of God. . . .
ROMANS 11:22

I

Just as the key text of Jesus' message is found in Mark 1:15, so one can say that the key text of Paul is found in Romans 1:16, 17.

> For I am not ashamed of the gospel: it is the power of God for salvation to every one who has faith, to the Jew first and also to the Greek. For in it the righteousness of God is revealed through faith for faith; as it is written, "He who through faith is righteous shall live."

These two texts proclaim the same good news in different ways. They both announce that God's final salvation is under way and available. Jesus testifies that the reign of God is at hand, is breaking through. Paul declares that the righteousness of God is now revealed, meaning the long-awaited manifestation of his faithfulness [1] to his supreme promises. As Paul uses the term "righteousness" here, and it is often so used in the

---

[1] "In Christ the consistency of God with himself—so grievously questioned throughout the whole world, among both Jews and Greeks—is brought to light and honored." So Karl Barth at this point in his great meditation on Romans. Barth calls attention to God's work in its perpendicular dimension alone and not in the horizontal dimension. "In Christ God offers Himself to be known as God beyond our trespass, beyond time and things and men . . . ," but here is no disclosure of God's righteous salvation in our ongoing actuality. *The Epistle to the Romans*, trans. by E. C. Hoskyns (London: O.U.P., 1933), pp. 40, 41.

Old Testament, the revelation of the righteousness of God means above all the enactment of his salvation.[2] So in the preceding verse Paul speaks of the Gospel as the power of God in saving action. Thus we find a clue whether in Jesus' message or in that of Paul: a Christian is one who should be able to testify out of his own experience and observation that the power of God is overwhelmingly at work bringing in the new creation. So indeed we find the earliest believers on trial before the Sanhedrin protesting, "we cannot but speak of what we have seen and heard" (Acts 4:20; cf. I John 1:1–4). And here too as in the case of Jesus and Paul the witness is borne by life as well as by word.

Thus there is no gulf between Jesus and Paul. They declare the same sublime fact—an unimaginable world transformation in course. As Paul develops his Gospel, it is true, he grounds it particularly in the cross and resurrection of Jesus. The dynamic action of God which Jesus had proclaimed has now evidenced itself even more signally and victoriously. Paul stands at a later point in the great transaction and has new evidence to offer: the passion, the resurrection and the operation of the Spirit in the church; but the good news and the warning remain essentially the same. Jesus sees Satan as lightning fallen from heaven. Paul sees the principalities and powers, the world rulers of this darkness, dethroned. The author of the Gospel of John sees the prince of this world cast out. It is the same message of redemption from bondage and evil, though in each case the salvation and the joy are for those—for that remnant—who dissolve their ties with the old age and assume the relationships of the new.

[2] See W. Sanday and A. C. Headlam, *A Critical and Exegetical Commentary on The Epistle to the Romans,* 5th ed. (Edinburgh: T. & T. Clark, 1902), pp. 24, 25, 34, 35. Also C. H. Dodd, *The Epistle of Paul to the Romans* (London: Hodder & Stoughton, 1932), pp. 9–13.

We have spoken of the modern misunderstanding of Jesus' message. In the case of Paul the misunderstandings are equally serious. It is all but impossible for men today to approach Paul fairly. Average Christianity which so generally takes its stamp from Paul has obscured if not betrayed him. There have been two chief types of distortion. One error has been to stereotype his teaching into a hard and fast dogmatic system, revolving especially around the theme of substitutionary atonement. Much of this is rightly grounded in Paul but wrongly formulated. In the absence of ample faith, the great images and concepts of Paul become shrunken and literal. Thus their truth becomes ambiguous or unrecognizable. The scandal which is indeed a real aspect of his antinomies takes on a second and unnecessary scandal of impoverishment. Another error is of an emotional rather than a dogmatic type. Here that appeal to the feelings which is an essential accompaniment of faith is overstressed and the revivalism which results is too exclusively individualistic. In either case valid elements in Paul are too much isolated or exaggerated. Impoverishment of faith leads to both distortions.

It must now be added that partly in reaction to these weaknesses, many groups of Christians have been alienated from Paul and have either evolved versions of the Gospel which lack his insights or have virtually abandoned Christianity altogether. Not infrequently one hears it said that Paul corrupted the simplicity of the Gospel. Certain confusions in the air as to Paul's relations to the mystery religions have aided and abetted these misunderstandings. Here it is not always sufficiently recognized first, that Jesus' own message was not as "simple" as is often supposed; second, that even before Paul the faith began to articulate itself with many richnesses; and,

third, that it could not be transplanted to the Gentile world
(our world!) without transforming itself and, indeed, sophisti-
cating itself.

What the layman does not ordinarily recognize is that the
Christian movement had already traveled a long way and
gone through a marked transformation before Paul's Christian
outlook was defined, and that Paul himself was shaped by and
had to address a different world from that of Palestinian
Jewry. Before Paul, Hellenistic-Jewish converts like Stephen
and Barnabas and the Christians in Antioch in Syria had
already modified the expression of the apostolic faith. The
diaspora Judaism out of which these men and Paul himself
came was different from that of Judea and Galilee, infiltrated
by elements from the wider Hellenistic world and still further
marked by the results of its long defense against this world.
This Judaism, moreover, had long been engaged in propaganda in the pagan world in which it lived. When Paul of
Tarsus, a convert to this new form of the Gospel, took up his
work among the Gentiles, he was far removed in many ways
from the pristine version of the faith, and the character of the
stage upon which he moved only accentuated this disparity
which as we know made for grave dissension in the church as
a whole.

The Greco-Roman provinces to which Paul carried the message still farther afield was, then, a wholly different theater
from that with which Jesus was concerned or the Twelve in
Jerusalem. The transition or transplantation involved here can
best be suggested for ourselves by the demands made upon the
Christian missionary today who goes to the great subcontinent
of India. Like India, the Hellenistic world of that time had its
rich profusion of religious, cultural and philosophical tradi-

tions and corporations, noble and base, often closely associated
with civic or social authority. In this congeries of cults and
patterns of life were to be found both allies and implacable
adversaries. For an approach to this exuberant and proud
oecumene the Hellenistic synagogue offered a bridgehead. It
was inevitable that the Christian faith should here take on
diversified and even technical thought patterns, many of them
as alien to us in their way as are the peculiar Jewish conceptions available to Jesus and to those who first proclaimed the
Gospel in Jerusalem.

It is understandable, then, that readers of the New Testament should observe an immense difference between the message of Jesus and that of Paul. Not only does Paul stand on
this side of the resurrection and read the significance of the
Nazarene in the light of it, in company here with Peter and
the other disciples. But Paul's outlook is still further distinguished by the factors of which we have spoken. However,
this does not justify us in saying that he was the real founder
of the church, nor in saying that there is a great gulf between
Jesus and Paul. For Paul had "the mind of Christ," that is,
he was in direct discipleship to him in what was of the essence:
the attitude, disposition and motivation; and, as we have seen,
Paul's message like that of Jesus was an announcement of the
Good News of the final divine operation.

Our chief handicap with regard to Paul is not, however, the
special categories in which his thought necessarily moves, but
rather the level at which it moves. Before we attempt to state
his message we must remind ourselves vividly of the context
out of which these first Christian documents were written, and
of the order of experience which they reflect. We revert again
to what has been said earlier about faith and its appropriate

language. Paul like Jesus is dealing with ultimates, and it is only as we crave an answer with regard to ultimates that we can enter at all sympathetically into his thought world, his issues and his convictions.

The prerequisite, surely, for adequate understanding of Paul or the New Testament or indeed any great religious faith is the knowledge of evil, especially moral evil, in the sense of a knowledge of its power and implication in life. It is not enough to have a conventional acquaintance with evil. Many men, indeed, have such acquaintance and have worked out for themselves a rationale of optimism or evasion sufficient to deal with it, unless even this limited recognition forces them into cynicism. The knowledge of evil includes, indeed, a vivid sense of the frailty of life, the miscarriage of human aspirations, the stubborn hold of cupidity, pride, violence and fraud. It is aware of the frustration of men's social and civilizing efforts, movingly summed up in the famous lament singled out by Renan:

> The peoples labor for the fire,
> And the nations weary themselves for vanity.
> [HAB. 2:13 (A.R.V.)]

It is aware of Vergil's poignant sense of tears in mortal things. But to understand Paul there must also be the sharpened sense of moral inadequacy over against the august holiness of the Deity and his austere and beneficent ends—the legacy (alone) of Israel. In this light moral evil in the self creates a sharper emergency, and evil in society calls forth a more fundamental reaction as in Augustine's outcry:

How woeful are you, O torrent of established custom. Who can resist you or when will you run dry? How long will you con-

tinue to roll the Sons of Eve into that vast and terrible sea in which even those who mount the cross scarcely escape drowning?
[CONFESSIONS 1.16]

The pagan or blasphemer who feels the acuteness of our moral predicament or who has an imaginative grasp of our human transiency is better qualified to understand Paul than many Christians. A sharp hunger and thirst after justice, which basically characterizes all men though it sleeps in many, calls for some such answer and some such revolutionary trans-saction as Paul postulates. Man's unappeasable craving for life, his instinctive and moral protest at the finality of the grave, require some such revealed mystery as the one he declares and interprets. So long as our proper self-knowledge slumbers in us, so long will the great themes of the Gospel disorient us. When these awaken, Paul's folly will appear wisdom, his great antinomies will become cogent, and even his bold wrestlings with free will, foreordination and cosmic destiny need no longer surprise us. Imperious and disabused demands require ultimate answers, and here a special language such as Paul's, appropriate to first and last things, is necessary.

II

Let us now seek to state Paul's message in his own terms and against the background of his total world view. Paul like Jesus declared that the men of his time were confronting the climax of the world's history. In the fullness of time God was initiating the new age, the new creation, which was soon to declare itself in the final judgment and renovation. In the fullness of time God had initiated that new creation by send-ing forth his Son, the New Adam, and through him was now restoring the broken order which prevailed by reconciling men and angelic powers to himself. The present phase of this work

H

of salvation in which both grace and judgment were offered
would lead on to the final transformation of the world into
unspeakable glory. For Paul history as it was then understood
was virtually at an end; it was worn out, its vitalities and
structural elements were passing away, "coming to naught."
The church stood in the midst of the great transition, in the
throes of the new creation, in a drama so intense and far-
reaching that it was best interpreted in terms of the conflict of
invisible cosmic agencies. The new order in birth manifested
itself in extraordinary powers, whether psychological or social,
and all the phenomena connected with it called for interpretation in transcendental or "mythological" categories. The coming of a new order always is a fatality for an old order, and
the negative dynamics of the Gospel were as stern as the positive dynamics were joyful. The Gospel was therefore both a
life-giving and a death-dealing incense:

> For we are a fragrance of Christ grateful to God in those being
> saved and in those perishing; to the one an odour of death that
> leads to death, and to others an odour of life that leads to life.
> [2 Cor. 2:15, 16 (Weymouth)]

To set the present occasion in a significant context Paul
employed the world story of the Old Testament with certain
elaborations it had recently received. Prototypes were found in
the great dealings of God with man in the past to illuminate
his present supreme action and to show its continuity with the
past. Thus Paul returns to David, to Moses, to Abraham, and
most significantly of all to Adam and the creation itself. Jesus
is first seen as the Messiah, the new David, of whose seed he
was born according to the flesh. The reign of the Messiah must
continue until God "has put all his enemies under his feet"
(1 Cor. 15:25; Pss. 8:6; 110:1). It is into this messianic

reign that we have been transferred, thus being delivered from the kingdom of darkness (Col. 1:13).

But the new situation also has its prototype in the Mosaic foundation.[3] Israel had been

baptized into Moses in the cloud and in the sea, and all ate the same supernatural food and all drank the same supernatural drink. For they drank from the supernatural Rock which followed them, and the Rock was Christ. [1 Cor. 10:2–4]

Yet the dispensation under Moses was one of death and a veil lay over the old Israel, a veil now removed in the new covenant which is one of the Spirit and of freedom (2 Cor. 3:6–18).

Again, Paul saw the new regime typified and forecast in Abraham who was justified by God on the ground of his faith. For are not the nations (the Gentiles) blessed in him through Christ the "seed of Abraham"; and are not the believers the true children of Abraham (Gal. 3:6–29)? Are they not "children of promise," "born according to the Spirit" like Isaac, and is not their mother the Jerusalem which is above and which is free (Gal. 4:21–31)?

In establishing these relationships with the past, Paul is not playing an obscurantist game of correspondences. He is making clear the consistency and irreversibility of the divine transaction with men. History as Paul sees it has been more than history. It has been an epic, a pilgrimage between heaven and earth, with its origin in the unsounded counsels of God, accompanied by prodigy and omen and aware throughout of its august outcomes. Faith throughout has perceived the im-

[3] "The 'redemption' of Israel out of Egyptian slavery had already become for the prophets a foreshadowing of the ultimate 'redemption' of the people of God from all the evils of this present age." Ex. 15:13; Dt. 7:8; Isa. 1:27; Jer. 31:11; Isa. 51:11; etc. Dodd, *The Apostolic Preaching and its Developments* (London: Hodder & Stoughton, 1936).

port and overtones of the episodes and vicissitudes, and its chronicles have necessarily been symbolic in character. Of these mysterious antecedents Paul avails himself to explicate the significance of the present.

But the full magnitude of Paul's conception appears in his final reversion to the creation itself. He could find no adequate antecedent and parallel for the dynamics of the world transformation which he saw in course short of this.

For it is the God who said, "Let light shine out of darkness," who has shone in our hearts to give the light of the knowledge of the glory of God in the face of Christ. [2 COR. 4:6]

And it is in this same connection that Paul gives us his most significant reading of the work and person of Christ. Over against the disobedient Adam of the first creation he sets the obedient new Adam of the new creation. Over against the man of the earth, earthy, subject to death, he sets the "man from heaven," the life-giving Adam; not the "living soul" of Gen. 2:7, but the quickening Spirit. From him springs now not only a new Israel but a new humanity. And by him who pre-existed the first creation and in whom all things were made, this new humanity awaits its full revelation as the sons of God. This work of restoration by the man from heaven involves his being made flesh and identifying himself with our utter extremity, so bringing to light both the goodness and severity of God.

Now however alien all this may sound to modern ears, we note at least that Paul sets his gospel of the cross in a grandiose world-historical frame. He talks in terms of Alpha and Omega. Religion, we have said, must come to terms with ultimate questions. If it uses symbol, fable, poetry, parable in combination with what we call history, it is only doing what men have always felt it necessary to do in conveying the overtones of experience as well as its immediate aspects.

III

There are two aspects of Paul's thought which deserve attention because they have no such prominence in the proclamation of Jesus himself. For one thing, of course, Paul lays great stress on Christ himself and especially on his cross and resurrection. It is through the cross above all that God had despoiled the principalities and powers which keep men in bondage so long as they belong to the old order (Col. 2:15). The present and realized kingdom of God is construed by Paul in the assurance that Christ is now Lord, and that he has dethroned the false rulers of the world (1 Cor. 2:6, 8; Gal. 4:3, 4; Col. 1:13). This centrality of Christ and his cross and resurrection is of course present in the Gospels. Like Paul, their authors and much of their tradition are post-Easter. Jesus' own view of the significance of his death in the coming of the kingdom is one of those areas of Gospel study about which we have too little evidence to speak with confidence. But it is clear that he believed he had a supreme role in connection with the great transformation and that his death was related to it in the deep counsels of God.

Another feature of Paul's formulation which has caused difficulty is his strong emphasis on the negative aspects of the Gospel. Not only is there for him a revelation of God's saving righteousness (Rom. 1:17) but in the very next breath and in the same terms there is a revelation of the wrath of God (Rom. 1:18). God's work is double-edged. "Behold therefore the goodness and severity of God," as Paul says in a more limited context (Rom. 11:22). How and where is the wrath of God revealed? Evidently in close relation to the revelation of his grace. In Rom. 1:18 ff. the "wrath" of God is exhibited in the moral anarchy and inhumanity of pagan society. All through the deformity and ruin he sees the operation of the divine judgment. But this judgment is inseparable in Paul's mind from the last judgment, and it is highlighted by the final salvation now in course. Where the light is brighter the shadows are deeper.

But we must add one further and more difficult observation here. For Paul the double revelation of God's grace and wrath, his goodness and severity, is seen also in the cross itself. It is not difficult for us to recognize the manifestation of God's grace in the cross, but modern theology and exegesis seek in every way to escape the teaching of Paul that God's judgment is also there exhibited. Yet it is part of Paul's deepest insight and ground of hope that in some sense Christ was subject to judgment; of course, in lieu of men. "For our sake he made him to be sin who knew no sin" (2 Cor. 5:21). "Christ redeemed us from the curse of the law, having become a curse for us" (Gal. 3:13); that is, Christ was subject to condemnation. We shall return to this, only remarking that Paul could not maintain our fellowship with Christ in his victory without also associating Christ all the way with our extremity.

The double aspect of God's action appears for Paul also in the preaching of the Gospel. As we have noted, the powerful word of God carries life to some and death to others. For the witness highlights, exposes, precipitates and crystallizes the human situation wherever it is preached. Thus there is a double-edged revelation of God's action throughout. Again, where the sunlight is brightest the shadows are darkest.

But this double aspect is not absent from Jesus' message,

though it is often overlooked. Never far from Jesus' compassion and elation is his awareness of the zeal of the Lord of Sabaoth who cannot defer his great ends or his rescue of the meek and the captive. Its background is found also in the Scriptures. It is the God of love of Hosea, who says,

Therefore am I unto Ephraim as a moth, and to the house of Judah as rottenness. [5:12]

For I will be unto Ephraim as a lion, and as a young lion to the house of Judah: I, even I, will tear and go away; I will carry off, and there shall be none to deliver. [5:14]

Yet this ravage is to the end of discipline and reformation. And ultimately the same God who sifts and scours the hearts of his people is the same as he who returns in mercy, as Israel comes to acknowledge:

He hath torn, and he will heal us; he hath smitten, and he will bind us up. [6:1]

And so in the case of Paul, the emphasis is on the positive side. The message is first of all good news. And the revelation of the wrath of God becomes a foil to the call to repentance. There are those who are troubled by what they call the pessimism of Paul. Paul is not a pessimist—that implies sentimentality. He has indeed the tragic sense, recognizing the moral impasse into which individuals and societies become involved and the inexorable character of moral consequences with their atrocious outcomes. The compounded error of men takes on a glacierlike momentum, becomes fate or *karma* for multitudes and takes on all the character of a veritable force of nature. If Paul uses graphic language of his time to illuminate the condition of men, we should not demur though we may object to those who would systematize it. Our chief difficulty is rather that Paul makes God responsible for these awful penalties. We should not let ourselves be put off by Paul's use of the archaic term "wrath" which by now in rabbinic parlance had become a technical term with little emotional connotation.[4] As C. H. Dodd shows, it stands for the reaction of God's holiness, though all personal connotations of the term are not lost. Sin, conscience, remorse have their importance and even obsessiveness for man just because a personal relation with God is finally involved.[5] When Jean-Paul Sartre says that "Hell is people," he means that the reaction of other persons to us conditions our self-consciousness and very being. This is even more true where God is concerned.

But Jesus and Paul and the New Testament as a whole see God's hand in moral penalties necessarily, since they believe in one God. It is easy to solve this question by insisting that since God is good we must set aside all talk of his "wrath" or his share in the great disasters that result from sin, private or general. But if we do that we dethrone God and are left with a world that has no sovereign. It is of the essence of the Christian faith that it is great enough to hold to and wrestle with the affirmation that God the friend and God the Stranger are one God.

IV

Having summarized Paul's message, we call attention now as we did in the case of Jesus to the reasons for its power in

[4] Cf. Dodd, *The Epistle of Paul to the Romans*, pp. 20–24. The translation, "anger" (Weymouth, Moffatt, Goodspeed) is thus misleading. R.S.V. retains "wrath."

[5] The extreme moral sensitiveness of man is due to the "personality" that inheres in the universe. It is because personality is the constitutive element in existence that from the youngest child to the most hardened adult we make mountains of the trifles of moral adjustment to other men. Why is discord in our personal relations so toxic to the soul? Because personality in the universe is so central. We seem to sense that to fail here is to fail in all.

his day. Paul too exploited the total resources, the heights and depths of his hearers' traditions. He touched their ultimate loyalties and possibilities to the quick. He convulsed their consciences and shattered their securities; in this aspect like the prophets:

Therefore have I hewed them by the prophets; I have slain them by the words of my mouth. [Hos. 6:5]

He made appeal to their sleeping hungers and faiths, and cast a torch into the explosive damps of the soul, of the Jew first and then of the Greek. It was in this sense that his message could be "in demonstration of the Spirit and power" (1 Cor. 2:4). The sacred history of God's people, its covenants and promises were brought into play. He made appeal to the total world picture and world story in the hearts of his hearers, both in respect to its origins in creation and its goal in the new creation.

When Paul dealt with Gentiles who were not nourished on the Scriptures, he appealed to their corresponding ideals and assumptions and the symbols in which these were current. The Greco-Roman world of the time did not, as in the case of the Jews, have a more or less common religious world picture. It did, however, have its dream of world salvation, its idealizations of a world savior and renewer. It had its bitter sense of cosmic bondage and cosmic tyrants. It too knew the *taedium* and flatness of a world that was old, and had its hungers for purity and immortality. It had its redeemer prototypes and its ceremonies of apotheosis. Paul knew how to lay hold of appropriate emotionally-charged symbol so as to speak to the soul and the heart of the Gentiles, and to activate their deepest hungers. It is the more astonishing that he was able to incorporate much of his Jewish-Christian scheme and symbols into his Hellenistic context. What he did here in redirecting the message of the Gospel to men with a different sense of existence is just what we have to do for men of our time.

Paul's message had power, in the second place, because, as in the case of Jesus but in a different theater, the hour was propitious. The fields were white to the harvest, not in the Empire generally but in certain strata. Not only had wise men from the East, Aramaic-speaking lands, been ready to bring gifts to the infancy of the new faith, but also certain Greeks from the West were disposed to inquire concerning it. Professor Toynbee has briefly characterized the timeliness of the Christian Gospel in this period:

The Christian Church itself arose out of the spiritual travail which was a consequence of the breakdown of the Graeco-Roman civilization. . . . The Graeco-Roman civilization served as a good handmaid to Christianity by bringing it to birth before that civilization finally went to pieces.[6]

V

No doubt many features of Paul's message of salvation and judgment, if taken at face value, are no longer meaningful or available to us today: the imminent world end; the cosmology with its heavenly powers, the origin of sin and death in Adam. His interpretation of the work and person of Christ also seems very alien to us at certain points. One mistake would be to reject Paul *in toto* because of these difficulties. A more common mistake is to attempt to make a hasty distinction between what we consider elements of abiding value and obsolete elements. If we attempt this we are likely to come out with a few outstanding passages of Paul's letters like 1 Cor. 13 and Rom. 12 together with a few great conceptions, letting the

[6] *A Study of History,* abridged ed., pp. 235, 236.

rest go as archaic and useless. This perverse way of dealing with Scripture or with the classics reminds us of one-time interpreters of *Paradise Lost* who read the epic for its occasional "purple passages" and who set aside its "outdated theology" as mere scaffolding. In this fashion they disqualified themselves completely from an understanding of the work and its organic character, and from an appreciation of either the thought or the art.

To grasp Paul's message we must first of all deal with it as a whole. As in the case of *Paradise Lost,* selected passages forfeit the greater part of their meaning if the great structural architecture of the entire work and conception is set aside. And where the ruling "ideology" appears outmoded to us we should make an effort to bring it to life for ourselves. In this way the well-loved aspects of Paul's writing will take on their full import. His paean to love and forbearance in 1 Cor. 13 will be all the more significant because it is grounded in the condescension of the divine love. His universalism will be better grounded when we recognize that its guarantees lie in the new race and family that take their rise in the cross. His great charter of freedom is spoken to those whose bondage has ended through their participation in the necessary redemption.

So far as Paul's message coincides with that of Jesus we do not need to repeat. God's work is manifest. The powers of darkness have been worsted. The new creation is in course. All the inexhaustible resources of the creator are on our side if we are on his. The work of the Spirit points toward the ultimate transfiguration:

> What no eye has seen, nor ear heard,
> nor the heart of man conceived,
> what God has prepared for those who love him.
>   [1 Cor. 2:9]

The realist asks if this is not a futile escapism as we look out on our world today and that world threatened by atomic war. We answer that this message brings home to us those possibilities of renewal in men that lie beyond our own assessment.

> For every static world that you or I impose
> Upon the real one must crack at times and new
> Patterns from old disorders open like a rose
> And old assumptions yield to new sensation;
> The Stranger in the wings is waiting for his cue
> The fuse is always laid to some annunciation.[7]

The message also recalls us to the faith and single-mindedness which through the church may be God's means for the preservation of the world generally from final catastrophe. It also reminds us of the great conception of the remnant in which the unhindered purpose of God can work itself out even after his severity, his strange work, is disclosed in calamity.

But Paul's version of the Good News does assign a special significance to the cross and construes the role of Jesus in new and in what many feel to be extravagant ways. Let us free ourselves from the legacy of those who have hardened or narrowed Paul's thought in this area, the dogmatist, the systematizers or the emotionalists. Let us then try to approach Paul's utterance at the level where he himself lived, with a deeply imaginative view of the human condition, at a depth where life and death, fate and freedom, are at stake, a depth at which the knowledge of evil shows us the insufficiency of all shallow proposals of salvation. Let us then be prepared to give its due to the kind of world symbol which Paul necessarily must employ to deal with such issues, symbols taken

---

[7] "Mutations," in Louis MacNeice, *Springboard* (Faber & Faber Ltd., 1944), p. 17. Used by permission.

over from his great heritage. Paul like Jesus before him uses the meaningful images and conceptions of his tradition to interpret the present and the future.

Finally, let us keep in mind the larger framework in which we have sought to interpret the faith of the New Testament. The emphasis in Paul's gospel, as in that of Jesus, falls upon God: his purpose, his working past and present, his goal. Paul is first of all affirming in his own terms what Jesus affirmed: the time is fulfilled and the kingdom of God is at hand, and adducing the evidence for it. From the time of John the Baptist on, a crater had opened in the deeper life of mankind evidencing prodigious creative impulses, and the whole New Testament is the record of how the nature of men and their cultural forms, Jew and Greek, were baptized, smelted and transformed by the visitation. This convulsion and renewal centered about the fate of Jesus of Nazareth who voiced its import and demand, and Paul was the one who showed most clearly how the powers of this great renovation were still mediated through him now in his risen aspect.

But Paul's chief concern is with the incomparably great exhibition of the divine activity in the age, and with an understanding of the divine strategy in history so illuminated. He leaves us free in our understanding of Christ himself. Paul is not interested first of all in what we call "Christology," or in distinguishing between the human and the divine natures in Christ. He is interested rather in what God effects by him and through him. And even here he has no one fixed doctrine. He offers now one and now another view of what the death of Christ meant, speaking at one time in Jewish categories, at another in Hellenistic and gnostic categories. He uses various titles or names for Christ and these are not empty honorifics or mere titles of honor. They indicate what he has accomplished and what he is still bringing to pass. "Messiah" (Christ) describes his role as agent of final salvation, in Jewish terms. "The man from heaven" identifies him both as the Jewish Son of Man and the Hellenistic Redeemer who overcomes the cosmic tyrants of sin, death and "flesh" and integrates a world marked by division. Other terms like "Lord" and "Son of God" take on these same associations each with their special connotation. If the world's moral and spiritual history was reshaped in this incandescent hour and a new door opened before the race, it was inevitable that that figure on whom the great transaction focused, however profound his own humility, should have been interpreted in many ways as the instrument of the wisdom and power of God.

VI

If then we seek to restate in modern terms Paul's message with respect to its emphasis on Christ, we could put it this way. Christ and in particular the cross was the door or narrow gate through which the race had to pass, and has to pass, to enter upon its fulfillment, or to enter upon the sublime Tomorrow which Jesus announced. Thus, so far as men's life on earth is concerned the coming of Christ initiates a new history. But it is more than a new history, it is a new creation whose power and whose evidences are such that its final fulfillment is not compatible with earthly conditions. In making the drama of Christ's life the center of history there is no essential difference between the proclamation of Jesus and the message of Paul. Paul narrows down the focus more exclusively upon the cross. But Jesus had made it clear that the new age with its fateful claims was emerging in his activity.

Arnold Toynbee has well pointed up the scandal for modern thought in the fact that the New Testament and the church have presumed to divide history at the birth of Christ, thus setting up "a dual back-to-back reckoning of dates B.C. and A.D.," to apply to the whole planet and to all the peoples that have ever lived. He cites it as an example of the egocentric view of history.

This dichotomy of historical time is a relic of the outlook of the internal proletariat of the Hellenic Society, which expressed its sense of alienation from the Hellenic dominant minority by making an absolute antithesis between that of the old Hellenic dispensation and that of the Christian Church, and thereby succumbed to the egocentric illusion (much more excusable in them, with their limited knowledge, than in us) of treating the transition from one of our twenty-one societies to another as the turning point of all human history.[8]

But we as Christians can do nothing about this scandal, though we recognize that many peoples have lived below the horizon of Golgotha, and have had their own ways of reckoning time. We recognize how foolish it was for the leaders of the French Revolution to begin their Year One on September 12, 1792. But nevertheless we believe it was right for the Christians to do this in connection with the birth of Christ, and later to read time backwards as well from this date.[9] But this judgment of ours is based on faith, a faith which the dispassionate student of ethnology and universal history cannot always be expected to share. We see in the cross the narrow gate through

---

[8] *A Study of History*, Abridged ed., pp. 38–39.

[9] "The reckoning of time *backwards* from the birth of Christ only became established in the eighteenth century." Up until then the reckoning of time B.C. "was not oriented to the birth of Christ but the years continued to be dated on the basis of older calendars of the world eras from the creation." Cullmann, *op. cit.*, pp. 17–18.

which the race must pass if it is to emerge from its period of
minority. Christ is the door through which the peoples pass
from law to freedom, and from division to unity. It is proper,
therefore, at least for this planet, that time be reckoned from
the birth of Christ.

Paul then sees in the cross the narrow gate of the new age.
How can we make this persuasive to men today? There are
two chief aspects of the Pauline doctrine of the work of Christ.
They are briefly suggested under the formulas, Christus Victor,
and Christ the sacrifice. Both are included under the larger
text from Romans 1:17 with which we began: the revelation
of the righteousness of God in the Gospel. The Christus Victor
theme has reference to his dethroning of the cosmic demonic
powers which keep men in bondage, a theme forecast in Jesus'
own proclamation. It is not easy to transfer the sense of this to
our modern categories. It is true that men today are increasingly aware that personal freedom is inexorably limited by
massive impersonal legacies, social forms and dogmas which
constitute fate for men and have as it were an existence of
their own. This is what Paul was talking about in his own
way in referring to the powers, principalities, and world rulers,
although his thinking about them pursued them right down
into their metaphysical roots. Now to say that God dethroned
these powers in the cross (Gal. 4:3–4, 8–9; Col. 2:15) is in
part to say that Jesus had been able in his own personal experience to emancipate himself from these tyrants, particularly
through his faithfulness to the point of death, and that this
emancipation was made available to his followers. Thus in
this respect the cross was the gate of the new age. By it Christ
destroyed the old "world" characterized by these thralldoms,
and man as he had been in this old world died with it.

Let us turn now to Paul's interpretation of Jesus as sacrifice or means of expiation (Rom. 3:25). This image cannot but mislead and trouble us if we set Christ over against God and think of him as appeasing or propitiating an angry deity. It is when we place the death of Christ in the general framework of God's action in history that the image becomes meaningful. It is the character and action of God that the cross discloses. In Christ God was himself at work re-establishing the broken order of life. But this means that within that broken order, in the historical process itself, God had to find means to come to grips with the miscarriage of the human story, both the established patterns of society which consecrated that miscarriage and the deeper generating impulses and appetites which sustained them. Thus the great renewal involved necessarily a tragic social conflict and rupture and the exhibition in a personal character of the motifs of the new age highlighted by his position at the point of conflict. The sin accumulated in social custom, attitude and value and the sin precisely of the "good" individual had to be challenged, brought to light, in a drama, a tragedy, with far-reaching significances drawn from the spiritual history of Israel. It is just because the moral and religious attainment of Israel was so great that the life of this people in this moment offered the possibilities of a divine action here of universal bearing. Jesus as both the pupil of, and rebel against, Israel could be one in whose fate the motifs of general human salvation could come to light. Since his death in this drama of judgment and renewal had such far-flung implications, it was natural and illuminating that it should be interpreted in terms of expiation, or rather a means of expiation set forth by God for men.

It is often said that since the Renaissance modern man feels

I

as his deepest need fulfillment of life, abundant life, carrying with it the great ideal of freedom. John's great texts on the abundant life and on the truth that makes us free are the favorite texts of many modern Christians. But we have here a misunderstanding. It is true that John Bunyan's Pilgrim flies from the City of Destruction crying out, "Life, Life, Eternal Life." But *that* life is life indeed, life unclouded and jubilant, because it is characterized by the renewal of innocency. The greatest hunger of men, modern or ancient, is not for abundance of life or even freedom in the common sense, but for the removal of the shadow and weight on the soul which mar our peace. Our greatest need is for the renewal of simplicity, of innocency, not the innocence of Adam or the child or the Greek but the innocency of maturity. Our moral failure and distress root back in our deepest being and in our fundamental orientation to God.

The innocency in question—not "peace of mind" or "peace of soul" but peace of heart– this condition of the heart which speaks in the Beatitudes and the Canticles and in the uninhibited confidence before God and man which marks Paul's letters, is not won by or granted to the individual alone, though many faiths see it this way. The matter is more difficult. Our lives are interwoven with those of our fellows, and our anxiety and guilt are interwoven with theirs. Purgation, therefore, requires a very profound social and historical transaction and a tragic one. Paul's reflection on the cross takes on meaning in this light. His metaphors and turns of expression may not always be available to us today. But we shall not find a solution for this need of innocency unless like him we relate the problem both to God himself and to our fateful human solidarity.

That man's deepest craving from the earliest dawn of conscience to the present is for reconciliation and peace is well brought out in a poem entitled "From Stone to Steel" by E. J. Pratt. The poem likewise suggests that all men's fumbling attempts at propitiation in a thousand cults and faiths point toward the meaning of Calvary.

> From stone to bronze, from bronze to steel
> Along the road-dust of the sun,
> Two revolutions of the wheel
> From Java to Geneva run.
>
> The snarl Neânderthal is worn
> Close to the smiling Aryan lips,
> The civil polish of the horn
> Gleams from our praying fingertips.
>
> The evolution of desire
> Has but matured a toxic wine,
> Drunk long before its heady fire
> Reddened Euphrates or the Rhine.
>
> Between the temple and the cave
> The boundary lies tissue-thin:
> The yearlings still the altars crave
> As satisfaction for a sin.
>
> The road goes up, the road goes down—
> Let Java or Geneva be—
> But whether to the cross or crown,
> The path lies through Gethsemane.[10]

Let us look now at the most difficult aspect of the matter as Paul states it. Christ on the cross represents us and bears our penalty. "For our sake he made him to be sin" (2 Cor. 5:21). "Having become a curse for us" (Gal. 3:13). "God put

---

[10] *Collected Poems*, p. 20. Copyright, 1945, by Edward J. Pratt. Used by permission of Alfred A. Knopf, Inc., and The Macmillan Company of Canada, Ltd.

[Christ] forward as an expiation" (Rom. 3:25). Many today shrink at such language. They can agree that Christ's love, and even God's love, is manifest and brought home to us in the death of Jesus. Here they stop. But this does not carry us far enough. The story of the cross so viewed may, indeed, move us to compunction and reformation of life through pity and terror. But how does it offer us any final guarantee of the triumph of love? It merely suggests to us two forces at work in the world, good and evil. In this case, it is true, love prevailed. But love is not thus exhibited as omnipotent over the roots of evil, or redemptive at the heart of life. Here is, therefore, no thoroughgoing and unqualified Good News. For Paul this definitive triumph is connected with the fact that Christ carried out his task as one fully identified by his love and humility with our human estrangement. Precisely by these he was "caught," as it were, in the solidarity of our need. By his cry on the cross, "My God, my God, why hast thou forsaken me," Christ voices the distance from God to which his involvement in our lot finally carried him, even while he accepted the will of God. But this involvement it was which furnished the opportunity for the triumph. Only so could the deeper infirmity in men meet with its cure and the bitter waters of the heart be healed. That this whole transaction and all the factors in it, even the sin of men, were overruled by God was affirmed in Paul's view that both his love and severity were brought to light in the cross, and that by a paradox judgment on men's sin was exhibited in the person of Christ. An old world under condemnation died with him and a new world was born.

The joy and gratitude of Christians surveying the mystery of the event which secured their deliverance has perforce always had recourse to these or similar pardoxes to convey its meaning. If we find Paul's language here difficult let us recall that he was using analogies familiar to the whole ancient world. We should by no means press his metaphors too far nor stereotype them. But neither let us take too superficial or too individualistic a view of sin and its remedy. And let us meditate the truth that the sway of moral evil is not finally disturbed by ideas but by hand-to-hand engagement and vicarious involvement and ordeal. Moreover, the evil that Christ met and overcame had a great generality, for his work was carried out at the crossroads of man's most significant moral and spiritual history. There man's situation in its darkest as well as its brightest aspects is exposed and dealt with. The working of God is revealed there in black and white, as nowhere else. And there God opened a door for men out of their impasse, a door opening upon a new creation and a new race.

VII

When all has been said that is said above, we realize that for many readers the case for Paul remains unconvincing. His understanding of the Gospel continues to mystify and repel men. And here it is not Paul alone but much of the New Testament that is challenged. All that has to do with atonement, with expiation, with the blood of Christ, all this emphasis upon his death and the related view that the believer must be crucified with Christ; this is an area of Christian thought which is a stumbling block for many. In one aspect, Christianity so defined seems to hang upon an isolated episode, indeed upon a kind of trick as men will say in their impatience. This is what is meant when the scoff is made that the Christians handily dispatch their sins upon a scapegoat and go their way with a light heart:

Your Jesus has wept; you may joke now.[11]

The more common charge, however, is that Christianity fosters an ascetic and morbid view of life. Wide areas of Christendom exhibit in art and cult an obsession with death and with suffering. Witness the dead or tortured Christs of Latin America and Spain, and the perverse strains, even orgies, of mortification and masochism which have recurred throughout the history of the church, both Catholic and Protestant. But we should not make Paul responsible for these aberrations. They can be traced often to pre-Christian outcroppings and atavism or to psychopathic impulses clothing themselves with Christian externals.

One remark may be made with regard to the theme of substitutionary atonement as found in Paul. The fact is that he intends what we may call a "representative" rather than a "substitutionary" view of Christ's death. When Paul writes that Christ died "for" me, he usually means not "instead of me" but "for my benefit." What makes this clear is that for Paul the believer dies *with* Christ. Thus it cannot be a matter of substitution or of a scapegoat. In another context, it is true, the analogy of the ransom of a captive or (very rarely) that of a sacrificial offering is brought into play by Paul and suggests substitution. But this motif, which has its natural source in our sense of gratitude for the undeserved grace of God, is dominated by the ruling conception of our participation with Christ in his death to sin and the law.

The objection on the ground of healthy-mindedness to Paul's imagery of expiation is understandable in the light of

[11] W. H. Auden, *The Age of Anxiety* (Faber & Faber Ltd., 1948), p. 124.

what many Christians have done with this imagery. Paul's
own teaching, however, read in its original context, is not thus
vulnerable. The issue finally is one of how seriously we conceive the predicament of moral evil and what kind of transaction or mediation we are prepared to envisage as indispensable
for its cure. The "liberal" is not always as superficial with
regard to this matter as is commonly charged. He recognizes
that individual and social sin require vicarious suffering if they
are to be overcome. He recognizes that the death of Jesus
added a final demonstration of his commitment to what he
lived and taught. He can understand the emergence of the
new community with its endowments and its testimony to the
glorified Christ as the proper sequel of such a life and death.

It is just here, however, that a main point is often overlooked. From our modern individualist standpoint we too
easily assume that the new movement could find its origin and
impetus in loyalty to the Nazarene and in the mutual love
which he had taught and illustrated. Such a view fails entirely
to do justice to the role of "ideology" in any powerful movement. The primitive community had an ideology (in the good
sense of the term) which, on the one hand, was related to the
deepest creative impulses of the faith, and which, on the other
hand, provided it with a distinctive picture of history and the
world by which it could define itself. The terms of this ideology
changed with time. But the varying formulations of the work
of Christ were an important aspect of this self-definition, without which the new group would have been inert and be-
wildered. And the formulations were potent just because they
borrowed familiar symbols and spoke to or contradicted inherited expectations.

Thus for Paul to declare that "Christ redeemed us from the

curse of the law, having become a curse for us" (Gal. 3:13), was a way of saying for Jewish ears that the righteousness sought after by Israel had found a wholly unexpected and paradoxical solution. And to repeat that "this cup is the new covenant in my blood," was to affirm the fulfillment of the promised redemption of Israel in connection with the death of Christ. The allusion to the blood of the covenant was a way of clarifying the relation of the church to God's dealings with his people on great occasions in the past.

Our difficulty with Paul's language has arisen because we have lost a sense of the living context in which he wrote. When doctrine is separated from life it becomes artificial and misleading. Paul's dramatic images of redemption had their vital soil in a living community.

To these struggling groups who had lost their citizenship in Israel or were exiles from pagan society these teachings were not "dogmas" or "tenets," nor were they merely a kind of theological poetry. By these symbolic accounts of emancipation and of Christ's role in it—accounts couched in long-familiar and relevant imagery—the new people set forth an understanding of themselves, of their situation and of their distinctive way of life. By them they accounted for their break with the synagogue, their abstention from the Jewish rebellion, their refusal of emperor worship, their repudiation of astrology and magic, their withdrawal from the civic and religious corporations of the Hellenistic cities. By them they justified the universalism of the church as against the Judaizers, the admission of slaves and women on an equal basis with freemen, and the break with licentiousness and individualism which were so characteristic of their environment. Thus the Christological images had a very practical this-worldly function. Theologians are as wrong in assigning them a purely spiritual and heavenly sense as they are in turning them into creedal shibboleths. They bore the same relation to the moral and even "political" life of the infant church that our democratic symbols and traditions do to our day-to-day decisions.

When in the Book of Revelation the twenty-four elders fall down before God and cast their crowns before the throne and sing:

> Worthy art thou, our Lord and God,
> To receive glory and honor and power [REV. 4:11],

the writer was not proffering an idle homage. Every Christian who read the book or heard it read knew that the Roman Emperor of the time, Domitian, claimed the title, "Our Lord and Our God": *Dominus et Deus Noster*. And when he wrote of Christ:

> Worthy art thou to take the scroll and to open its seals,
> for thou wast slain and by thy blood didst ransom men for God
> from every tribe and tongue and people and nation,
> and hast made them a kingdom and priests to our God,
> and they shall reign on earth [REV. 5:9–10],

the writer was both writing sedition in his semiclandestine work, and accounting for the origin of a new and universal empire. Moreover, the words of this strophe rest upon the liturgy of the Jewish synagogue and carry an implicit contrast between the redemption of this universal people and that of the Hebrew slaves in Egypt.[12]

In analogous ways the titles which Paul assigns to Jesus of Nazareth have implicit social and political implications as over

[12] Cf. Lucetta Mowry, "Revelation 4–5 and the Early Christian Liturgical Usage," in *Journal of Biblical Literature*, LXXI, II, June, 1952, p. 80.

against both Judaism and Rome. Jesus is both Anointed King and Lord of lords. His reign has an effectual bearing on the actual order of the world, present and future, and on many of its social features: patterns of family and group, calendar, occupation, custom, ceremony and even citizenship. When Paul writes that "our citizenship is in heaven" he is speaking of the final source of the Christian brotherhood; he is not denying the earthly corollaries of this new *patria*.

Thus redemption as Paul understood it had what we would call a political and cultural meaning. The new community was delivered from the low-ceiling, from the penitentiary-like existence, from the strait-jacket constraints which character- ized the authoritarian atmosphere of the time. Both Jew and Gentile were subject to inherited patterns which stifled spon- taneity and dwarfed the spirit. Paul talks about bondage, captivity, tyrants, subjection to "principalities and powers." It is quite clear that he is first of all concerned with bondage to sin. But he does not mean personal sin or sinful habit alone. He means sin as it is organized and transmitted in what we call culture and what he calls the "world." The bondage he has in mind includes the reign of various constraints occasioned by sin, giant authorities that derive their power over society in connection with sin: above all "law" in its impersonal aspects, especially the Jewish law, but also pagan conventions and conformities, idolatrous cults and ceremonies sanctioning the pride and lusts of men and blinding men to the sovereignty of God. The Christians had broken through this low ceiling of spiritual tyranny, had emerged from this suffocating barrack- room atmosphere which cowed the soul, and it was through Christ that this had come about. It is true that they were still subject to the existing, often arbitrary, political powers. Paul did not deny Caesar his jurisdiction for the time being. But they had escaped the fears and appetites that gave Caesar power over men's souls.

Interpreters of the Bible through the centuries have understandably been absorbed with the subjective and personal aspects of salvation. The saving of the soul, repentance and forgiveness, justification of the guilty, dissipation of the black cloud of death and new birth into eternal life—all this was taken to be the heart of the Good News. Lutheranism and pietism especially laid the emphasis here and have influenced all other forms of Protestantism. But what we are concerned with here is not so much our later conceptions of salvation but the mistaken way in which the New Testament writings have been interpreted. It is not recognized that Jesus wrestled with the miscarriage of a national calling and set his witness and life against very concrete structures of social and cultural evil. It is true that he called for individual repentance and taught such parables as that of the prodigal son. But his all-encompassing mission had to do with a new Israel, a new temple; and the heavenly symbols he used for these should not blind us to the corporate renewal of God's people that was involved.

Similarly, it is not recognized that Paul, for all his emphasis on individual justification and the resurrection of the believer from the dead, was concerned with a great epochal revolution of the race. The fact that he did not allow a long period for the culmination of this process is beside the point. He saw the Gentile world entering into the heritage of Israel. The redemption wrought by Christ had this social and historical sense. In Christ the gulf between Jew and Greek was bridged and a new humanity was founded. The redemption meant a dispelling of age-old delusions, enchantments, tribal idolatries which

had held sway over the souls of men, and which had as much
to do with social and racial cleavages as with what we call
sin or vice. If Paul spoke of the expiation offered by Christ
for sin or said that while we were yet sinners Christ died for
us, he never thought of this atonement for individuals apart
from the general world renewal that furnished the setting. To
say that "Christ our Passover is offered for us" was to connect
the private redemption with the public, the personal with the
social, as the allusion to the historic deliverance of Israel makes
clear.

The older interpreters of Paul have thus done us the disservice of isolating his doctrines from their life situation, thus
rendering them artificial and excessively otherworldly. This
has obscured our understanding of the early Christian movement. But the greater disservice done us by much of the
Pauline theology has been in connection with our view of the
Gospel for our own time. Redemption is not something that
can be confined within the four walls of a sacred edifice. It is
not first of all a transaction of the soul with God at the moment of baptism or in the Eucharist, or in some hour of
private meditation and ecstatic foretaste of eternal life. Redemption involves the tyrants of the forum, the market place
and the hearth; the false dogmas of the state and the economy;
the idolatries and spells of social traditions as they appear in
inflexible conventions and complacencies; and the insidious
authorities of unreason and passion that speak through propaganda and the mass media. Here operate the principalities
and powers that are potentially dethroned by Christ. Individual and social salvation go together. Paul's converts were
the beneficiaries of a tremendous social emancipation as well
as of a spiritual rebirth. His doctrine of atonement ceases to

be unreal wherever we discover its bearing on these continuing tyrannies and whenever we attain in Christ to actual mastery in these death struggles both for ourselves and for our fellow men. It is only our firsthand experience of the difficulties involved and the costliness of victory which can authenticate to us the terms that Paul uses.

V

the Johannine witness

Now is the judgment of this world, now shall the
ruler of this world be cast out.   JOHN 12:31

This is the victory that overcomes the world, our
faith.   1 JOHN 5:4

I

The Fourth Gospel makes an especial appeal to many modern
men outside the churches and to many Christians who find
Paul a stumbling block. There is a curious paradox here because this Gospel goes beyond Paul in many ways that might
be expected to trouble contemporary readers. We need only
mention the sharply exclusive claims made for Christ. "None
cometh to the Father save by me." ". . . apart from me ye
can do nothing." "All who came before me are thieves and
robbers." There are other features of the work which have
aroused question: the alleged "limitation of love" to the Christian society; the harsh attitude toward the Jews collectively;
the portrait of Christ in terms of "the power and the glory"
rather than in terms of humility and humanity; the representation of his mighty deeds as signs rather than as works of
compassion.

Yet there are many who find this Gospel specially congenial.
It appears to be more universal, more free of outworn Jewish
imagery, more akin to general religious truth as we find it in
comparative religion or in the "perennial philosophy." The
Fourth Gospel appears to have been less vulnerable to the

great succession of shocks to the Bible that have come from
the rise of modern science and rationalism, from the work of
Copernicus and Darwin, and from modern historical method.

It is a fact that the time scheme and picture of history that
we find in the Old Testament, Paul and the Synoptic Gospels,
with the doctrines of creation, fall and last judgment—all this
has come to seem unreal for modern thought. Readers today
do not find themselves at home with the basic plot of *Paradise
Lost* any more than they do with *The Divine Comedy*. But in
the Gospel of John this Jewish-Christian time scheme has been
perceptibly modified and spiritualized. This Gospel speaks
more of present judgment than of last judgment and more of
eternal life than of the kingdom of God. It is more characterized by mysticism than by eschatology. It is the gospel of
the spirit and of the inner life. The incarnation seems to be
the dominant theme rather than the atonement. And even if
modern readers object to the idea of the incarnation, it is
always possible here to treat it as a myth or an allegory and
to look upon the "idea of Christ in the gospels" (Santayana)
as a sublime symbol of a universal truth.

If, furthermore, we can thus free ourselves from the outworn language of Jewish antecedents, are we not then better
able to come to terms with the religions of the East? Does not
the Fourth Gospel perhaps offer us the basis not merely for an
ecumenical theology congenial to the Greek and Russian
Orthodox Churches, but for a world faith! As Ernest Benz
has written in discussing the one-sided development of the
theology of Paul and of the New Testament in the West:

The dominant themes of Orthodox piety are not justification,
but deification, sanctification, rebirth, new creation, resurrection
and transfiguration. On these grounds the whole development of

life in the church took on an entirely different character from that in western Christendom.[1]

Orthodox theologians like Florovsky are calling us back to the thought of the early church Fathers before the juristic emphasis of the West had established itself, and missionary statesmen in India have long told us of the appeal of John for the Orient.

A recent writer, whom we have already quoted, calling attention to the disintegration of the typical world view of Christianity and the "smashing of the traditional myth-history" connected with it, asks whether Christian thought is not moving toward a new depreciation of time, in effect a new epoch of otherworldly mysticism.

We seem, indeed, to have turned in the direction of the Orient. In the East, especially in India, men have never taken history and time very seriously or felt them vividly to be real. Buddhism and Hinduism, in particular, have consciously elaborated and used myths as symbols of eternal truths quite without concern for historical accuracy. By losing its focus on time and history, by concentration on eternity and myth, Christianity might, in fact, be able to absorb the Orient into Christendom more easily than has proved possible with its traditional historical-activist emphasis. . . . The Orientals, who have long claimed that our Occidental activism is a symptom of religious immaturity, may therefore be complacent at the prospect that out of the present religious crisis, the greatest since that of antiquity from which Christianity itself emerged, there may well come a more quietistic and contemplative form of Western religion.[2]

We raise these questions with regard to the Fourth Gospel not only because they suggest the importance it may have in the theology of the future, but also because they suggest the

---

[1] "Das Paulus-Verständnis in der morgenländischen und abendländischen Kirche," *Zeitschrift für Religions-und Geistesgeschichte,* 3 Jahrgang 1951, Heft 4, p. 297.

[2] Lynn White, "Christian Myth and Christian History," in *Journal of the History of Ideas,* Vol. III, No. 2, April, 1942, p. 158.

real dangers it runs of misinterpretation. This Gospel arose in part precisely as a weapon against heresy. It would be ironical if today it should through misunderstanding become an accomplice of modern heresy. It arose in part as a weapon against gnosticism. It would be lamentable if today it were to become the occasion of a modern gnosticism whether of an orientalizing type or any other. There are signs today that in our zeal for the meeting of East and West we may seek a common denominator in mystical pantheism or in idealism and call it Christian. On the other hand, we should rejoice fully in the opportunity that Johannine theology rightly understood offers us for contact with Eastern religions, with Eastern Orthodoxy or with trends in the modern Western outlook. It is no doubt true that the predominant Paulinism of our Reformation tradition is due for both a renewal and an enrichment. From the time of Tertullian and Cyprian the Western church has identified itself almost exclusively with the legal and juristic side of Paul's thought, in keeping with its Latin and Roman antecedents and temper. The theology of the Reformation only confirms this observation. It is those parts of Paul's letters concerned with the Jewish law and with justification that have been decisive. But an equally significant aspect of Paul's gospel is found in 2 Corinthians and elsewhere, an aspect highlighted in Orthodox traditions and more akin to Johannine piety. Benz discusses this in the article cited and calls attention to a more integral view of the apostle to the Gentiles.

Albert Schweitzer has well expressed the relation of the doctrine of justification to the mystical theology of the apostle Paul when he writes: "By beginning with the teaching concerning justification by faith the true understanding of Paul's thought-

K.

world was rendered impossible." [3] The doctrine of justification is only one way among others by which to convey the content of the gospels. [4]

But if the Fourth Gospel is to aid us today in a more relevant definition of the faith, it must be more correctly understood than is often the case. Two current misunderstandings will illustrate the matter. There are perhaps no texts in the New Testament that are more frequently used in certain circles than these from this Gospel:

And you will know the truth, and the truth will make you free.
[8:31].
I came that they may have life, and have it abundantly.
[10:10].

Too often these passages are employed without recognition of the true sense of the terms used in their context in this Gospel. Life, abundant life, eternal life in this context refers to that kind and quality of life mediated by the Good Shepherd who lays down his life for the sheep and who is the door of the sheep. The abundant life in question is theirs who enter into fellowship with God as his love reaches them through the love of the Son. This kind of abundant life should not be confused with other kinds. A man can lack the Four Freedoms and still have the kind of abundant life of which John speaks, though this should not be taken as a depreciation of the Four Freedoms. Economic securities, social justice and opportunities of personal fulfillment are legitimate corollaries and outcomes of life as here understood, but they do not exhaust its significance.

Even more glaring is the misconstruction often put upon the

[3] *Die Mystik des Apostels Paulus* (Tübingen, 1930), p. 215.
[4] Cf. Benz, *"Das Paulus Verständnis . . . ,"* p. 307.

first passage. It is a question first of knowing what the words "truth" and "freedom" mean in this Gospel. The same verse ("If you continue in my word . . .") shows that truth here refers to the import of Jesus' instruction, that is, his Christological claims. And the immediately succeeding verses show that the freedom in question is freedom from sin. It follows that it is the Son who makes free, and free indeed. Of course, it is to be granted that the preacher can give a somewhat larger extension to the sense of a text. But the basic meaning should be kept in mind. Unfortunately, this saying as to truth and freedom is used in the tradition of rationalism in a sense almost diametrically opposed to that which it has in Scripture.

II

So much for some of the issues presented by this Gospel. We turn now to an examination of its teaching. We must inquire whether it is possible to identify here the same total faith and the same good news of the divine action which we have found in Jesus and Paul. In any case we shall wish to scrutinize the peculiarities of this evangelist's formulation of the Gospel. We shall be interested again to observe what kind of symbols are employed in this so different a writing, and the reasons for their potency in certain circles. Lastly, we shall consider the modern relevance of the Johannine witness.

We should give full recognition to the distinctive features of this Gospel and its outlook. It was only with difficulty that it won general acceptance in the course of the second century and so came to be numbered with the other three in the fourfold gospel canon. It is a very different kind of composition from Matthew or Luke-Acts. Considerable parts of John have the character of meditations on eternal life and fellowship with

God rather than that of an evangelical history. The discourses of Jesus are, as it were, lifted out of time. Some scholars have concluded that they had been used liturgically before they found their way into the present Gospel, just as the beginning section of the First Epistle of Peter is thought to have been a baptismal charge. Others have recognized in them or behind them a series of poems like the Odes of Solomon celebrating in gnostic fashion the divine Messenger, the Light-Bringer who descends into this world of darkness for our redemption. In any case, these meditations were at some time incorporated into a gospel framework so as to present the career of Christ in an eternal setting. Thus a work was produced that resembles the other Gospels. Like them it represents a combination of history and interpretation, a combination of earlier and later traditions. Like the other Gospels it sets forth the good news of the divine working, of the final salvation, and calls on men to repent and believe. Here is another expression of the world-shaping faith of the young Christian movement to put beside the proclamation of Jesus and the gospel of Paul.

We need only summarize here what is commonly recognized. The conception of eternal life *here and now* largely supersedes the conception of the new age to come in the future. The conception of a present automatic judgment largely supersedes that of a future forensic last judgment. The conception of Christ's return after his death in the form of the Spirit largely supersedes that of his parousia on the clouds. All in all, the Jewish view of the new age and the consummation at the end of a time series seems to be abandoned in favor of a somewhat Platonic vision of God, a present transfiguration into an eternal order. In short, we have a sublimated eschatology, or, indeed, as some have ventured to say, mysticism instead of eschatology. As C. H. Dodd puts it:

The fact is that in this gospel even more fully than in Paul eschatology is sublimated into a distinctive kind of mysticism. Its underlying philosophy like that of the Epistle to the Hebrews, is of a Platonic cast, which is always congenial to the mystical outlook. The ultimate reality, instead of being, as in Jewish apocalyptic, figured as the last term in the historical series, is conceived as an eternal order of being, of which the phenomenal order in history is the shadow or·symbol. This eternal order is the Kingdom of God, into which Christians have been born again, by water and the spirit (iii, 3–8).[5]

It is in keeping with this revised or different view of history that Jesus is interpreted in ways congenial to Hellenistic syncretism and that Jewish terms like kingdom of God, Son of Man, resurrection, fall into the background or are given a greatly modified sense. Dr. Ethelbert Stauffer holds that John's work rests on a philosophy of being. The recurrent theme, *"in the beginning was,"* used of God, the logos, and even of the prince of this world, and the presentation of light and darkness as metaphysical realities, underlie and determine the evangelist's understanding of what comes to pass in the historical scene. It is precisely the conflict of light and darkness which comes to issue in the Gospel drama and has its cosmic solution in the judgment effected by the incarnate logos both at his crucifixion and at its sequel, the eventual separation of spirits at the last day.[6] In this setting it is understandable that the horizontal time scheme recedes in importance though

[5] *The Apostolic Preaching,* pp. 109–10. See discussion of this passage by W. F. Howard, *Christianity According to St. John* (London: Duckworth, 1947), pp. 123-24.

[6] *New Testament Theology* (London: S.C.M. Press, E.T. 1955), p. 42. An ultimate dualism is excluded, however, by John 1:3; and 8:44 denies to Satan any final reality as Stauffer recognizes.

"John is also a theologian of history like all the thinkers of early Christianity."

Another way to grasp the significance of John's emphasis is in terms of "realized eschatology." Here it can be simply put by saying that in his own way this Gospel brings into the center of the picture that present aspect of salvation which is already recognized in the proclamation of Jesus and the gospel of Paul. This is the special emphasis of C. H. Dodd in *The Apostolic Preaching*.[7] W. F. Howard echoes Dodd's exposition of this theme. In the teaching of Jesus as represented in the other Gospels,

> The powers of the age to come are already on the ground as an army of occupation. So the disciples of John the Baptist were to tell their master. In the same way the "signs" in the Fourth Gospel tell their tale of the same powers in the hands of Jesus. The exultant cry that went up, according to St. Luke, when the Seventy returned with the report of their mission, "I beheld Satan fall as lightning from heaven," is recalled by the Johannine, "Now is the judgment of this world, now shall the prince of this world be cast out." In each case the present victory sounds the death-knell of diabolic pretension.[8]

Howard adds: "The decisive battle has been won, but the warfare is not yet accomplished." But in the Fourth Gospel it is often maintained by other scholars that the warfare *is* already finally accomplished and that realized eschatology is the only kind of fulfillment there is. It is in this sense allegedly that the writer uses the phrase, "the time is coming, *and now is*" (i.e., "when the dead will hear the voice of the Son of God" [5:25]). It is in keeping with this view that Rudolf Bultmann and others have excised as glosses those passages in

[7] Pp. 109–10.
[8] Howard, *op. cit.*, p. 117.

which the second coming and judgment at the last day are referred to.[9]

III

When, however, we have made all due allowance for the mysticism and for the "now" rather than the "then" of salvation in John, we still must recognize that the basic view of history of the Old Testament and of Jesus and Paul is not abolished. The case here has been effectively stated in the volume of Howard to which we have referred, in the chapter entitled "Eschatology and Mysticism." Much of the most significant recent writing on this gospel supports it.[10] The Fourth Gospel has specific references to the last day, the final judgment and the general resurrection, and these passages are integral parts of it. Conversely it may well be that the four Paraclete passages, with their somewhat different outlook, represent a late stratum in the book. Their effect is to eclipse the second advent of Christ at the last day and to substitute for it his return in the spirit. Howard draws attention, moreover, to the eschatological significance in John of the use of certain terms like Son of Man, kingdom of God, the tribulation, and to the contrast of the present and the future age, and other

---

[9] 5:28–29; 6:54, etc. Cf. Bultmann, *"Die Eschatologie des vierten Evangeliums,"* in *Glauben und Verstehen* (Tübingen, 1933), pp. 134–52; also *Das Evangelium des Johannes* (Göttingen, 1950).

[10] Cf. H. E. Weber, *Eschatologie und Mystik im Neuen Testament* (Gutersloh, 1930), ch. V; Ernst Percy, *Untersuchungen über den Ursprung der Johanneischen Theologie* (Lund, 1939); Cullmann, *op. cit.,* p. 89; Stauffer, *op. cit.,* p. 42 f.; Ph. H. Menoud, "Le Problème Johannique, III," in *Revue de théologie et de philosophie,* xliii (1931), pp. 80–100. Menoud in a review of Percy's work writes: "Thus John keeps the drama of salvation within the limits of the relations of Creator and creatures. He remains within the line of action of the Old Testament, Judaism and the emerging church," *ibid.,* xxx (1942), p. 172. Cf. also H. Odeberg, *The Fourth Gospel* (Uppsala, 1929), pp. 69–71.

details. The conclusion is unavoidable. The Jewish "plan of salvation" is not abolished. But the point of view of the author is such that certain aspects fall into the background.

The kinship of the Johannine writer with Paul and with the synoptics must be asserted in another respect. Even where he uses terms and conceptions drawn from a pagan background: light, life, truth, vine, shepherd, etc., even where he uses such contrasts as light and darkness, truth and falsehood, in all such cases we can note how all these elements are conformed to the Christian message. With regard to these dualistic contrasts, for instance, Dr. Ernst Percy has shown how different they are from corresponding cosmological conceptions in Mandaeanism and hermetism.[11] With regard to the figures of the vine, the shepherd, the bread of life, etc., Eduard Schweizer has shown how far the Johannine use departs from their mythological use elsewhere. In the Mandaean literature, for instance, the vine was conceived as a real living vine, source of the mystic's life, and personified. The light was an actual divine substance, also personified. When Jesus defines himself as the "true" bread and the "true" vine or "good" shepherd, it is in polemic contrast to all such gnostic redeemers.[12] Here it is to be noted that the true bread and true vine, etc., are not to be taken in a Platonic sense.[13] Here we have another indication that the mysticism of this Gospel is not to be confused either with Platonism or with an Oriental gnosticism. There is a mysticism in John as there is in Paul. But it is a mysticism entirely controlled by the evangelical history and the cross. It is a historical mysticism, a faith mysticism, an agape mysticism.[14]

---

[11] *Op. cit.*, Erster Teil: Der Dualismus.

[12] E. Schweizer, *Ego Eimi* (Göttingen, 1939).

[13] Contrary to Dodd's view at this point, *The Apostolic Preaching*, p. 110. Cf. E. Schweizer, *op. cit.*, pp. 131–38.

[14] Cf. Weber, *op. cit.*, pp. 184–88. Bultmann in his article on the

We reach this conclusion, then, with regard to the Johannine view of salvation that despite all its special features it insists in its own way upon the concrete historical significance of the gospel events and assumes the Jewish-Christian plan of salvation. In a discussion of the biblical terms, "age," "this age," "the age to come," and of the Jewish view of history in general, Dr. Ethelbert Stauffer writes as follows:

We should pay due attention to the fact that even those New Testament writings which betray a thorough acquaintance with the world of Greek culture, cling fast to the conception of the apocalyptic age (Ephesians, the Pastorals), and even develop it (Hebrews). They were well aware that with this conception they had something distinctive and revolutionary to say to the Greeks. They [the Greeks] could interpret the face of the earth and the heavens; but they could not read the signs of the times (Luke 12:56; Matt. 16:3). . . . History for the Greeks is only an appearance within the cosmos. For the early Christians, on the other hand, the cosmos is only an appearance within history. *The Greek hearkens to the eternal harmony of the spheres. The men of the New Testament hearken to the footfalls of universal history [den Schritt der Allgeschichte].*[15]

This statement applies to the Gospel of John even though we recognize that its acquaintance is less with Greek culture than with Oriental syncretism. In this work, too, the Gentiles are taught that history is the locus of revelation, and that they should listen there for the steps of the Almighty.

We find, therefore, in John also the characteristic message

---

eschatology of the Fourth Gospel referred to above shows that there is no cosmological dualism in it; the "world" is not viewed in terms of matter or fate; there is no dualism of body and soul; no speculation on the fate of the soul; no idealism or humanism, for life is communicated only by the Father and the Son on condition of obedient hearing, not esoteric knowledge; "abiding in Christ" means faithfulness in response to the revelation. The validity of these distinctions of Bultmann is not affected by his existentialist interpretation of the Gospel in other respects.

[15] *Op. cit.*, German ed. p. 60 (our tr., italics); E.T. p. 76.

and common faith of the New Testament as we have found it in the proclamation of Jesus and in the message of Paul. This work, too, announces that in fulfillment of his long plan God, working hitherto, is now bringing his plan to its consummation; through his Son breaking the power of evil and inviting all men into the fellowship of the sons of God and eternal life. This formulation like the others rests upon a total faith, that is, the certainty that God is sovereign over *all* things (apart from his word "was not anything made that was made"). This formulation also insists that God discloses himself in men's historical life, driving this point home especially in connection with its testimony that the word became flesh and that Christ's death was a real death. The central drama, moreover, again receives its significance from the place it occupies in the context of first and last things, and its nearer setting in the working of God in the Old Testament. Faith again has its total vision of the world and of history, indeed of cosmic history. Furthermore, this Gospel in what concerns its organization is patterned very closely upon the early kerygma as found in the sermons in Acts and elsewhere. The setting in the Old Testament, the work of the forerunner, John the Baptist, Jesus' ministry of word and healing, his death, resurrection and anticipated return all have their portrayal here, though with modifications.

IV

Once we have noted how much John has in common with the rest of the New Testament, once we have stressed its real concern with history, once we have thus set limits to interpretations of it in terms of mysticisms, Platonism or gnosticism, we can be quite candid as to the ways in which it is *sui generis*.

This Gospel is written from a very special angle of vision. It is astonishing that so diverse a tradition appeared so early as the time in which its sources were in the making. The peculiar perspective from which it is written results in quite a remarkable *displacement* of those elements held in common with the rest of the New Testament. We are looking at the same landscape but from so different an observation point that we at first find it difficult to recognize the familiar features. This difference can of course be accounted for by the different milieu in which it was produced, by the special group for which it was written and by the special apologetic aims of the evangelist. But these all add up to something more decisive. We are in danger of misjudging this Gospel unless we are clear on this point. There is a tendency, indeed, among some scholars to mark down its value very drastically (quite apart from the question of its value as a source for the life of Jesus).

The point to insist on here is that there is a very great simplification and concentration in the approach of this evangelist and those on whom he depends for his tradition. The focus of his attention is narrowed and directed selectively upon the central issues of the Gospel story so that much of its more general context is passed over or foreshortened. This concentration also explains the universality of the work. It is "every man," all flesh, that is involved here. God loves the *world* and Christ lifted up draws *all men* to himself. This is not incompatible with the concern for the narrower circle of the disciple in the farewell discourses and prayer. It would not be correct to say that this evangelist sees the Gospel story *sub specie aeternitatis* for that suggests a Platonism alien to him. Eternal life in John does not mean a timeless state or the "eternal Now." But it is true that he sees that story from a certain re-

move. This is not a close-up view such as at least by compari-
son the other Gospels give us, thus affording us a greater
impression of realism and immediacy. The author of John
stands at a sufficient remove from the great drama so that he
is able to see and concentrate on its essential pattern. This
makes for a degree of abstraction, and even for a degree of
unreality there where the spiritual insights or abstractions are
imposed upon actual episodes in the narrative. But the supreme
marvel of the writing lies in the way our life in time is related
to ultimates, and in the sense it gives us that the days of our
years can and do receive ineffable meaning from the divine
immanence as well as from the divine transcendence.

Viewed in this light, many of the questions that arise with
regard to this Gospel disappear. The "monotony" of style and
thesis; the large place given to abstraction and allegory; the
extraordinary perversity assigned to Jesus' interlocutors; the
systematic way in which the condemnation of many is assigned to predestination; the generalized identification of
Jesus' antagonists as "the Jews" as though he himself were not
a Jew; the strange presentation of Jesus' prayer as though it
were not true prayer but spoken for the benefit of the hearers
(11:41–42); the fixing of interest on the true interpretation
of the sacraments rather than their institution; the portrayal
of Christ in terms of the "power and the glory"; and the interest in his teaching on the divine fellowship rather than on
concrete moral topics; all such special features of John are
understandable when we take into account the perspective and
concentration of interest of the author.[16]

[16] Santayana speaks very well of these matters: ". . . the constant use
of these abstract terms in *John* chills a little the underlying warmth and
the tragic inspiration of the narrative. They also destroy the lifelikeness
of the speeches. . . . The image of Christ in these parts becomes corre-

V

The author's inclination to see the New Testament message in these terms is unquestionably conditioned by his setting. The background of this Gospel has of late been very much clarified. There was a type of religious outlook especially in Syria and Asia Minor which had evidently penetrated into Judaism, gnostic in character and specially influenced by Iranian conceptions. John both in ideas and in style reflects elements that come to expression in later Mandaean, hermetic and gnostic writings. Evidently in this period wide circles of men found their religious needs answered not in the ordinary forms of Judaism, nor in the mystery cults nor in the Greco-Roman religious philosophies. Existence was pictured in terms of a twofold order of light and darkness, truth and falsehood, life and death. This world was created by the powers of darkness but man's soul had had its origin from the light-world. It could only be saved by a redeemer and revealer sent from above. He spoke of himself as the light, the shepherd, the water of life, and invited men into fellowship with himself. Conceptions of this kind found their way into Judaism, relating themselves especially to its apocalyptic forms and its sectarian groups. One strain of Christian missionary preaching learned how to make its appeal to men of this religious outlook. But it had of course to baptize all such conceptions and correct them by the Old Testament heritage and by the faith and message of the Gospel.

---

spondingly pale and impersonal. He seems to be addressing all mankind, or only an abstracted part of the soul, rather than his living hearers. On the whole, however, these beginnings of theology in *John* are far from destroying the graphic and topographically distinct impression produced, or the evangelical character of this Gospel. Essentially the book remains a prophecy, an announcement, and a challenge." *Op. cit.,* p. 32.

Benjamin W. Bacon well characterizes the procedure of this evangelist. The career of Jesus had for him a world-wide significance.

He applies to it the current religious conceptions of the contemporary Hellenistic world. Such a career is held by him and others to bridge the chasm between earth and heaven. The eternal Source of light and life is thought of as descending from heaven to earth through mysterious channels, finding voice, and ultimately embodiment, in human individuals, and ascending again to its heavenly home. One who thus descends to men and again ascends to the larger life of heaven may "open the kingdom of heaven to all believers." He becomes a Son of Man on whom the angels of God ascend and descend, as in the vision of Jacob.[17]

Here we return then to a theme we have urged throughout. These religious symbols were powerful in the Johannine form because they meant so much to those who had cherished them in their pre-Christian context. The conception of the Word, the contrast of above and below, of light and darkness, the figure of the Light Bringer, the images of the tree of life and the water of life—to use these cherished terms was to engage the deepest imaginative and spiritual life of such hearers, and to offer them a faith that dealt with existence as a whole. The Christian faith is, indeed, a denial of the wisdom of all forms of paganism at vital points. But its challenge to paganism (and secularism) is more or less effective according as it relates itself intimately to the realities and symbols in which life has hitherto disclosed itself to men.

Certainly the Fourth Gospel revises and corrects the pagan conceptions which it utilizes. The chief point is that they are incorporated into the world historical scheme of the Bible. To

[17] *The Gospel of the Hellenists* (New York: Holt, 1933), p. 354.

God is assigned the creation of darkness as well as of light. The bondage of men to error is assigned pre-eminently to sin rather than to ignorance. Christ, the Redeemer, is identified as the *true* vine, and as the *good* shepherd. The eternal life to which he admits is grounded in love and characterized by love. Knowledge (*gnosis*) is no longer esoteric but means apprehending and being apprehended by the love of the Father, just as "believing" means commitment to that love. The "concentration" of John's message is upon the love and glory of God as they come to their most intense expression in the cross. It was here that the judgment of the prince of this world was actualized, in this historical event. And for us too the victory that overcomes the world lies in our faith directed toward this event.

But if this author is seen at work transforming the pagan conceptions about him, he also saw the need of restating the current version of the Gospel, in this milieu. The message as taught, for example, by Peter, whose general character is reflected probably in Mark and the other Synoptic Gospels and in the sermons in Acts, did not and could not touch or search men's hearts here as it had elsewhere.

The whole drama of redemption needed to be viewed from a loftier standpoint. . . . Especially indispensable were a revised demonology, and an eschatology greatly spiritualized and purged of the Jewish nationalism which clings to it even in the earliest Epistles of Paul.[18]

x

But this consideration leads us on by a natural transition to the question of the relevance of the Johannine message today, and we cannot do better than begin with Bacon's argument on this point.[19] He notes that the situation of the church in our

[18] *Ibid.,* p. 306.
[19] *Ibid.,* pp. 307–8; 354–55.

time calls imperatively for a modernized interpretation of the great doctrines of the apostolic message and of Paul. For men of the twentieth century, he writes, accustomed to think in terms of world religions and schooled in the disciplines of Greek thought, men for whom Jewish conceptions of the after-life have become alien, and among whom different views of God and his relation to the universe and ourselves prevail; for such men the Johannine version of the gospel has much to offer.

The modern man is ready to believe that the human qualities of faith, love, devotion, seen at their highest in Jesus, are not of the earth earthy. But to appreciate that the eternal nature of God, ever making for righteousness, ever working for man's redemption, is here revealed incarnate, there must be a deeper foundation than the portrait drawn from the reminiscences of Peter, however glorified by visions of the Son of Man. The modern Christian has long founded his faith, and will continue to found it, on the eternal, indwelling Christ of Paul. . . . Something corresponding to the Logos doctrine of John is indeed indispensable to the maintenance of the historic faith in the rational atmosphere of today.[20]

Bacon rightly analyzes the situation today so far as concerns multitudes of men. We know of course that there are countless orthodox Christians in all lands who find no difficulty still in thinking in terms of the Jewish-Christian apocalypticism and adventism which we find in the Synoptic Gospels, the Book of Revelation and other parts of the New Testament. But Christian preachers and apologists need to recognize the more characteristic modern outlook in the West just as missionaries to India need to take account of prevailing views there; and in both cases certain Jewish categories in the early faith are today

[20] *Ibid.,* pp. 307–8.

a liability. As we noted at the beginning of this chapter, for vast numbers of men of our generation the traditional myth-history of our religion has been "smashed," and this bears particularly upon elements of the Jewish world view incorporated within it.

To turn to the Fourth Gospel, however, is not to find an easy solution for this problem. After all, even in this Gospel, as we have sought to show, we find many of the essentials of the Jewish-Christian conception of history and the world. It is not just another book of mysticism which can be isolated from the rest of the New Testament and claimed by anthroposophists (Rudolf Steiner) or modern Platonists or spiritualists or orientalizing movements. Personality in God, the doctrine of creation rather than emanation, the moral aspect of knowledge, the particularity of God's revelation to Israel, the doctrines of the incarnation, the atonement, the resurrection of Christ and the final judgment at the last day—these are all in this Gospel and it is not permissible to view them as mere poetry or as particular expressions of universal truths.

If it be true that the biblical world picture and history picture have broken down, then this Gospel is involved if not to the same degree as the other Gospels and Paul. But this generalization with regard to the biblical world view is too sweeping. There are, indeed, in the contemporary world many who reject the Christian faith altogether, and who naturally reject with it its picture of existence, its symbols of creation, fall, judgment, etc. We are more concerned here with those who reject these elements in the New Testament because they suppose that they must be viewed as literal prose fact. But in our second chapter we have sought to show that the language of great faith cannot and should not be viewed as literal in this

L

sense, and that Jesus' apocalyptic imagery of the kingdom of God and Paul's interpretation of the cross, while they affirm realities in history and beyond, are symbolic in character and should so be interpreted and reinterpreted. As a matter of fact, the average man knows this when theological or other fashions do not mislead him. Neither the rationalist on the one hand nor the literalist on the other can for any length of time convince the layman that the Bible is a book of prose.

Thus we believe that the Bible's picture of the world story and of God's dealing with men is far from being broken down, though there is certainly a great deal of confusion and bewilderment. What is needed is helpful interpretation and restatement. If this is done in immediate relation to contemporary need, the old-world symbols will turn out to be assets rather than liabilities for faith. In the preceding chapters we have sought to show how such restatement can be carried out.

But it still remains true that the Fourth Gospel has certain advantages for us today. Protestantism since the Reformation has been predominantly Pauline, and Pauline in the partial sense indicated by his juridical categories. Where it has declined it has often been characterized, strangely enough, by moralism. But whether moralistic, dogmatic or emotional, the prevailing types of Protestantism have not encouraged the kind of inwardness and simplicity that the Christian mysticism of the Fourth Gospel represents. To those large modern groups who are alienated from prevailing types of sectarian Christianity this Gospel comes with fresh appeal. Its concern with Christ known as the Spirit and with man's destiny in terms of eternal life speaks persuasively to men today.

This Gospel, together with the First Epistle of John, moreover, sanctions a Christian freedom in all that concerns church, office and sacrament which is needed today. These writings were not only antignostic but they were also anti-ecclesiastical. The authority of the apostles is meaningfully subordinated to that of the "beloved disciple" who is a symbol of the true witness of faith in any generation, whether an eye-witness of Christ or not. In the eyes of this evangelist the twelve apostles gathered about Christ are representative of the believers that shall come after rather than authoritative media-tors of an authoritative tradition. This view is quite contrary to that we find in Matthew, Acts or the Pastoral Epistles, for whom church office and true doctrine are traced back to apostolic authority. So far as concerns the sacraments this Gospel omits their institution. This evangelist is primarily con-cerned with correcting misunderstandings as to their character and efficacy. The whole matter is clearest in connection with the role here of the Spirit. Whereas in this period the function of the Spirit was becoming identified with church office and with sacrament, for John the Spirit is still free. It is given to all Christians and to the community as a whole, rather than to office or stated rite. It is the Spirit alone which purifies, makes forgiveness of sins effective, or authenticates tradition.

Revelation for him is no completed event to be preserved in the salvation-institution of the church. . . . It is the present Christ that legitimizes the tradition, and not vice versa.[21]

The Gospel and First Epistle of John are written from a point of view which runs counter to the rise of the early Catholic church as the forecast of the latter appears in Acts, the Pas-toral Epistles and elsewhere.

[21] Ernst Käsemann, "Ketzer und Zeuge: zum johanneischen Verfasser-problem," *Zeitschrift für Theologie und Kirche,* 48 (1951), 3, p. 310. See pp. 302–11 for this whole theme.

Thus this Gospel can serve the renewal of Protestantism today both as a rebuke to sectarianism and as a norm of true catholicity. It assigns primacy to the present dynamic activity of God without forfeiting the significance of the saving historical events of the past. The categories in which the Gospel is presented are available today if their symbolic character is recognized. Many of the figures in which John speaks of eternal life and its imparting are so simple as to need no restatement. Bread, water, light, etc. immediately evoke our primary needs, and at more than one level. The shepherd suggests our need for security; the vine is the symbol of man's demand for joy as well as for nourishment, of

that savor of life in which we sense our bond with the great stream of life, and which we recognize in all domains, the artistic, the political, the intellectual.[22]

John teaches us that these goods which are "the objects of all the questing and travail of the world" are mediated to us through the eternal Word by whom all natural goods were first created, and through whose coming in the flesh their true import is conveyed.

The announcement of eternal life sums up all these goods. The old world of darkness is judged. The ruler of that world is cast out. That world was a world in which men had sought these goods blindly and perversely, and had thus enslaved themselves to tyrants and false gods of whom "the prince of this world" was the symbol. But the love of God had found a way to judge that world, to dethrone its prince and to make all things new. And from that bondage we also are delivered. "This is the victory that overcomes the world, even our faith."

[22] E. Schweizer, *op. cit.*, p. 130.

VI

conclusion

After our study of the New Testament faith as we find it set forth by Jesus, Paul and the Fourth Gospel we may well return to the fundamental questions raised in our first two chapters. In Chapter I we considered the special circumstances today to which any formulation of the New Testament message must address itself if it is to receive a hearing. That message must commend itself as relevant to men's this-worldly historical experience; it must not be escapist and compensatory. Man's whole indivisible nature, material and spiritual, social and individual, must be dealt with. But a relevant faith must also invoke ultimates and speak of Alpha and Omega; otherwise it cannot pretend to offer redemption in any final sense. We also noted how contemporary biblical study has opened up an understanding of the Christian faith which meets just these kinds of demands.

In Chapter II we recognized the problem created for us by the old-world conceptions in terms of which the New Testament faith is presented. We urged that faith has its own particular language, a symbolic and mythopoetic language, and that such language conveys truth and knowledge. It is just because the early Christian faith involved affirmations of an ultimate and total kind that symbolic expression was imperative. Moreover, the dramatic pictorial vehicles of expression—reflecting so vividly the most passionately held ideals and hungers of the ancient world—afford a better testimony to the concrete significance of the faith than general abstractions ever could. The religious "poetry," "midrash," "myth," if these terms may be used, serve to convey both the scope of faith and its human relatedness. It is true that if the church binds itself to the letter of such symbols it falsifies their original sense and vitality. On the other hand, to discard the symbolic elements in favor of the supposed perennial truths they contain is also to forfeit the full significance of the faith.

In the last three chapters we have had opportunity to observe various aspects of the language of faith in the New Testament and to explore the problems of its modern relevance more in particular. Attention to dominant features in the outlook of Jesus, Paul and the Fourth Gospel has, indeed, obliged us to acknowledge the alien character of many basic assumptions and conceptions. We have not sought to evade the difficulties. At the same time we were led to recognize the potency of the great images and pictures used in the Scriptures for rallying the devotion of men of the time and for dramatizing the profounder alternatives before them. By such emotionally-charged symbols as those of the kingdom of God, the last judgment and the victorious Redeemer the life of men and the course of the world could be presented in such a way as to "make sense" in the light of ancient expectations. Thus also deliverance out of a hopeless impasse could be effectively offered, not only to the individual but to the nation or the New Israel, and not only in an otherworldly but also in a here-and-now sense. For if an otherworldly consummation was assumed, this had its present temporal counterpart. It was not only that a proleptic grasp was assured here and now upon a dawning new age or world to come, but that a new form of human community was actually available with very practical benefits both material and spiritual.

But we also had occasion in these three chapters to explore various aspects of the problem of modern relevance. In none of the three instances, Jesus, Paul or the Fourth Gospel, does there appear to be any insuperable difficulty for our contemporary use of the ancient symbols employed. They must, indeed, be constantly quickened by sensitive and inward grasp, and by illuminating interpretation. But such conceptions and figures as those of the creation and the judgment, the struggle of heavenly and demonic forces, the Redeemer and his sacrifice, the incarnate Logos and the Holy Spirit, all such are available to us without hindrance or danger if their essential character is recognized. We see the proper procedure frequently when a wise preacher applies a scriptural text for his hearers, illuminating it by effective modern analogy, but also deepening their understanding of the contemporary issue by the setting it receives in the light of the text and of Scripture generally. A similar fruitful interplay is found in the procedure of the modern theologian. What brings the Scripture and its symbols to life is the faith of the interpreter, a faith at grips with contemporary adversaries and circumstances. It is out of the throes of one who wrestles with the immediate human situation that the Bible is understood and not out of a sheltered piety however well instructed. The traditionalist may evade the difficulties present in the Bible by sheer docility, but at the same time he never really encounters its full present import and demand.

The extraordinary feature of our contemporary situation is that many of the unchurched today, just because of their exposure to tragedy and crisis, are finding the biblical imagery meaningful. The agnostics and secularists who are turning back to the church today are attracted by the profound interpretations of the human lot found in the Scriptures and in the liturgy, dramatized as they are in the great images of the Fall, the redemption and the judgment. If the modern rationalist rejects myth, the modern artist acclaims it. If the modern liberal seeks to strip off the legendary and mythopoetic strata in the Bible, the postliberal but not illiberal believer affirms it.

In doing so it is imperative that confusions be avoided. A postliberal understanding of the New Testament is not one that returns to orthodoxy unless orthodoxy be understood in terms of the free kerygmatic tradition. The postliberal does not deny his liberalism. It is the liberal movement which has helped to free him from a false or verbal orthodoxy. It is the liberal movement which has made possible form criticism of the Gospels and all those new insights into the beginning of the church which underlie our present more constructive grasp of the New Testament. The postliberal cannot be a biblicist. But neither can he sympathize with that kind of New Testament theology today which minimizes the historical aspect of the origins of the faith. The postliberal still believes that revelation comes and came *through* human circumstance and not only *to* it. If a scholar as a man of faith so stresses the arbitrariness of the Word of God in the beginning of Christianity as to discount the human context in which God spoke, he in effect is telling the theologian and preacher today that Christianity has little to do with our everyday life. If, on the other hand, he recognizes that the coming of Christ and the success of the mission to the Gentiles signalized the operation of God through and in demonstrable historical and cultural circumstances, he is telling the modern theologian and preacher that the issues of Christianity today are inseparable from the great cultural and moral problems of *our* society and *our* world.

The leading New Testament figures and writers worked with ideals and images in which were caught up the deeper hungers and frustrations, loyalties and apostasies of men. And these ideals and images were not religious abstractions but cultural and even political legacies. They were like emblems and banners in which the lives of countless men in many generations were reflected. It was through these kinds of community symbols, evocative of fateful memories, covenants, callings and hopes that God became real, and that he spoke and blessed or judged men. Figures like John the Baptist, Jesus and Paul not only proclaimed the great issues of their times by appeal to such symbols but crystallized these same issues in their own personal lives and fates. One main theme of these chapters has been that Christianity whether in its origins or in the present cannot be abstracted into a "religious" dimension but relates itself to the total life, indeed, the public life of men. Such life in all periods represents conflict and drama, fateful collision of rival social patterns and community ideals. The really significant religious forces of a time are to be found at the point of such conflicts. It is here that the work of God is to be known most potently. The proclaimers and bearers of his cause will still be those who recognize and interpret these main dramas in the life of an age and who can speak to the hearts of men in terms of the Christian alternative.

In a world like ours among whose legacies the biblical faith has so considerable a part, the defense of the Gospel will relate itself to the actual contemporary scene, the vital choices, the historical dilemmas. To preach only to the individual in terms of his soul, or to formulate a Christian ethic in terms of a remedial philanthropy, to espouse a theology of revelation of a sheerly transcendental and individualist character, to present Christian evangelism in the form of a biblicist revivalism, to use biblical language as though it were a sacred idiom sundered from all the travail out of which it arose, to forget the human, yes "secular" drama out of which men shaped their "religious" terms and images and to which faith always again directed its message; all such procedures represent attempts to short-circuit the operations of grace. Evidently redemptive Christian power is not absent from such partial versions of the Gospel, and some of them represent understandable reactions against earlier deformations of biblical truth, but all of them are incomplete. They miss the point of one or other of the two following insights: first, that our human experience in its most mundane and even irreligious particularity, as a realm of second causes, is the order in which grace operates; and second, the symbols used in the past as the vehicles of revelation convey its quality and meaning better than our dogmatic or rationalized equivalents.

This does not mean that bold attempts may not be made in any generation to go behind the language of faith of the New Testament in an effort to convey its import more adequately for the new day. So long as the proposed contemporary equivalents are controlled by the original faith and by the Christian experience of the present, this is a necessary aspect of Christian witness and defense. In fact, it is a necessary way of retaining contact and encounter with the Gospel. This process always goes on, consciously or unconsciously, especially in new times and regions, and is invaluable if only because it thwarts the perennial tendency of the church to assign extrinsic authority to formulas whether of belief or rite which were appropriate to a given period of the past.

The values, risks and implications of such reinterpretation can be well illustrated by the proposal of Professor Rudolf Bultmann to which we have already alluded. Here is one contemporary attempt to get behind the language of faith of the New Testament so as to commend the Gospel more vitally to the minds and hearts of men today. As we have seen, Bultmann finds that the message of the first Christians was formulated in "mythological" terms in two senses. On the one hand, the world view of the first century is presupposed, and, on the other hand, the current mythological images of Redeemer and redemption are used. That is, we have a Ptolemaic cosmology together with a Jewish apocalyptic view of the course of time. And we have an account of salvation enacted in this setting which depends on existing conceptions of a pre-existent being who becomes incarnate so as to effect the deliverance of believers through their identification with his representative and victorious struggle against the powers of darkness.

Now Bultmann has made it clear that he recognizes the value of the mythological elements in the preaching of the early church. His German term, *Entmythologisierung,* which means the freeing of the message from myth, has a negative connotation which he has deplored. He has always insisted that he does not propose to eliminate mythical features in the Gospel with a view to identifying a historical remainder. He is concerned rather with distinguishing a perennial kerygmatic or confessional aspect from the mythical, and the former is understood as the living word of God addressed to faith. His purpose is then constructive not negative. He offers a positive restatement of the New Testament faith which will gather up

all that is conveyed in its formulations including the mythological elements.

This task is a justifiable one, indeed, a necessary one. The
issue then becomes chiefly one as to the modern framework of
thought or ideology chosen to serve as the basis of the restatement, and as to the adequacy of such an ideology for the communication of the Gospel. The final test will be whether the
rich meanings which inhere in the New Testament symbols
are carried over into the new formulation with all their proper
normative significance. It is at this point that Bultmann's procedure has been questioned, and this query applies more generally to any similar attempt to find modern equivalents for
the rhetoric of faith in the New Testament.

We turn then to examine this scholar's method more closely
as one illustrative of the more general problem. The framework he uses is that of contemporary existential philosophy.
This outlook is rapidly becoming more widely known in this
country, and it is possible to grasp what is involved here without a technical discussion. The peculiar advantage of this
framework is that Bultmann is able to concentrate upon what
is indeed central to the Gospel, namely, the role of the will, of
choice, of decision; indeed, upon that level of personal existence where man is free, or can free himself from the bondage
of his past and of the "world" in which he is caught. Here
this interpreter has no difficulty in showing that the New
Testament everywhere presents man in this light and with
this responsibility and this opportunity. The mythology of the
old and the new ages, the drama of redemption, its presentation in terms of the death of the old man and the resurrection
of the new man, all this belongs to the heart of the Gospel and
is congenial to statement in existentialist terms. Of course, the

part played by faith is essential but the object of faith here, the work of God in Christ, does not on Bultmann's view require the mythological language of the New Testament. God's word, the word of the cross, has its own convincing power apart from all such borrowed imagery.

The Fourth Gospel serves the purpose of this author especially well.[1] Not only do we have here an example of how the Jewish apocalyptic mythology is largely dispensed with, and within the New Testament itself, but its own peculiar mythology drawn from Hellenistic syncretism offers itself readily to a modern existentialist interpretation. In his commentary on John, Bultmann identifies a discourse source in which, on the pattern of current Gnostic oracles, the Revealer and Redeemer offers himself as a medium of life and truth. It is particularly these discourses (*"Offenbarungsreden"*), assigned to Jesus by the evangelist, which lend themselves to this modern reformulation. Here Christ offers the believer not a future life in the world to come but immediate "eternal life." This eternal life, moreover, is not to be understood as mystical union with God in a pantheist sense. It means a continuing relation of responsibility and "faith." In his commentary on John, Bultmann's exegesis of the allegory of the true vine and the branches (pp. 406 ff.) develops this point. The Christian faith maintains the idea of *personal* relation to God, of ever-renewed responsibility and decision, and there is, therefore, always an element of "distance" in the fellowship of man and God, or of man and Christ.

The great truth of the New Testament which this formula-

[1] Cf. "Die Eschatologie des vierten Evangeliums", in *Glauben und Verstehen* (Tubingen, 1933), pp. 134–52; *Das Evangelium des Johannes* (Gottingen, 1950); *Theology of the New Testament*, Vol. 2, E.T. 1955.

tion safeguards is that of our emancipation from the bondage
of the old age, from the "world" (both without us and within
us), and freedom for a future that is God's future, for possibilities that are God's ineffable possibilities and therefore not
restricted by any determinations which we as men may lay
down. Those, on the other hand, who belong to the "world"
and cling to it deny themselves this true future. For the world
"holds on to itself," affirms its own glory, and chooses its own
false and anxious securities rather than the security in faith
alone which God offers. The choice between the two kinds of
security and future is presented to men by the coming of
Christ and that presentation renews itself continually in the
preaching of the word.

Here we have the doctrine of the continued "contempo-
raneity" of Christ who is present to all generations in the word
of revelation and preaching. "The true sense of the contem-
poraneity of the historical datum Jesus is not found in memory
and reconstruction but in preaching." [2] Or again, "Life is not
a given or an *experience* but refers to the fact that the present
'Now' is determined by the word where it is heard in faith."
That is, eternal life is not something we *possess* but something
which is continually given to us on condition that we die to
self and the world. Thus we keep open the unlimited possibilities of the divine action for ourselves ("God's future").
The farewell discourses in John develop these themes, according to Bultmann. It is true that they employ mythology and
mysticism for the purpose. But the relation of the believer to
Christ and to God remains one of "distance," that is, the
pagan mysticism underlying the borrowed myths is set aside
by the way in which this Christian Gospel revises them. The

[2] *Glauben und Verstehen*, p. 146.

crisis continues for the disciple. To "abide in him," i.e., in Christ, is not to be taken mystically, but refers to faithfulness to the revelation and the new commandment of love. Bultmann holds that John's presentation of the Gospel is closer in such matters to the essential message of the historical Jesus than any of the other Gospels.

It is this scholar's view that the characteristic outlook of men today disposes them to an understanding of the Gospel in existentialist terms. Idealistic philosophies have lost their hold. The terms which moved our fathers to devotion have become empty, and too often call forth a bitter derision. What the mass-man of today knows best is a sense of bondage, and what he craves is an area of freedom and personal affirmation. This the Gospel offers. For here men can find the strength to put off the tyrannies of the age. "The revelation of salvation [i.e., in the preaching of the cross] restores the lost possibilities of the creation." It will be recalled that in our attempt to state the deeper significance of Jesus' view of the kingdom as the promise of an ineffable fruition of life, and as uttered out of a level where man is made and unmade and where the world is made and unmade, we were saying essentially the same thing.

Here is an example, then, of how an attempt can be made in modern terms to offer a constructive reinterpretation of the language of faith. Bultmann's formulation at least highlights much that is at the heart of the Gospel and makes possible an effective impact of that Gospel today in many quarters where more traditional versions have lost their appeal. What needs further attention here, however, is the unresolved question as to how far the original language of faith comes into its own in Bultmann's proposal and how far its rights should be safeguarded in any such restatement.

Any modern philosophy will have its special liabilities when used as the framework for the presentation of the Gospel. In the case of existentialism it is in the areas of the doctrine of God and of the creation that the liability is greatest. Existentialism understands man and his situation, but leaves the role of God and the realm of nature in the dark. But the Bible's mythology of creation must be given its rights. Moreover, existentialism also fails to give any adequate account of *how* men are delivered from bondage into freedom, and even such a Christian version of it as Bultmann offers has great difficulties. This deliverance is, of course, assigned to the work of God in Christ. But to understand this and to proclaim it cogently we surely cannot forego the mythopoetic categories of the New Testament. Bultmann, however, underlines the obsolete character of these symbols. Moderns often find little reality in the New Testament conceptions of the Messianic deliverer, the incarnation of the Word, or expiatory sacrifice. Indeed, the history of doctrine shows that the church tends to freeze such images into objective stereotypes and so forfeit the true meaning of encounter with God which they originally mediated. This scholar, therefore, would have us rest our Christian witness to the saving events upon the pure word of faith divorced from the "mythology." But we believe, in the light of our discussion of the rhetoric of faith, that such a procedure forfeits our best means of truly conveying the significance and reality of the cross and the resurrection.

If, as we have stated it, the pictorial representations used by the first Christians embodied vital insights into God's working drawn out of long wrestling with experience, and if in their application to the work of Christ they convey the rich overtones of significance found in that work, we can ill afford to relinquish them. We must go further and affirm that for all their strangeness these symbols are inseparable from the message, the kerygma; they themselves mediate the revelation and are valid carriers of the wisdom and power of God. It is in part because he cannot accept this, presumably, that Bultmann limits the revelation to the kerygma itself. But thus to separate the word from the human vehicles in which it is uttered seems to us to involve a depreciation of all historical-cultural life, to withdraw the divine operation from it, and to have the unfortunate further consequences for modern Christians of leaving them without any basis for an adequate ethic.

Disagreement with Bultmann's position centers especially about his understanding of the crucifixion and the resurrection of Christ. If the mythological interpretations of the cross offered in the New Testament and drawn from ancient views of expiation or victory over cosmic powers are set aside, its significance is then grasped only in faith's existential encounter as the believer dies and rises with Christ through repentance. The cross then is an event which we know only in our sharing of it. But surely this approach tends to divest the crucifixion of its historical reality. Rather than a public event which like others had its psychological and social context and influence, the cross becomes as it were a type or paradigm; that is, a type of that crucial moment for all men in which God offers us death to our worldliness and awakening to our true possibilities.

The resurrection is likewise spiritualized, it is charged, since it is seen as only the obverse of the crucifixion and not as an event in itself.[3] It is especially in connection with the Fourth

[3] Cf. Regin Prenter, " Mythe et Evangile," in *Revue de Théologie et Philosophie,* Vol. XXXV (1947), p. 60.

Gospel's understanding of the cross as itself the moment of the exaltation and glorification of Christ that Bultmann plausibly follows this line of thought. That is, the gnostic elements in John furnish a natural bridge to an existential understanding of the whole revealing event.[4] Criticism of this view of the resurrection of Christ has been drastic and cogent. It is at this point especially that Bultmann has had to pay too high a price for the main *schema* he has borrowed from existential philosophy, with all its advantages. Prenter's theme, no doubt overstated, is that Bultmann falls into psychologism. The crucifixion and the resurrection become phenomena in the soul. And this carries with it a deformation of the Christian conception of God, who, no longer operative, sovereign and compassionate, becomes a mere function of the existential decision.[5] As Prenter says, mythology in the sense of symbolic statement is essential in religion, and when an attempt is made to forego it we land either in an arid metaphysics or in psychologism.

But such criticism goes too far. Bultmann has made it clear that he gives full recognition to the event of the crucifixion under Pilate as the historical origin of the faith.[6] While on his view the resurrection of Christ is not a separate event nor a historical event, he gives full recognition to the resurrection faith of the first believers. It is his insistence on the deepest significance of cross and resurrection which leads him to depreciate the forms and categories in which that significance was first interpreted. Any modern view of the resurrection narratives will be sympathetic with his procedure here in what concerns their legendary character. Moreover, his existentialist

---

[4] Cf. P. H. Menoud, *op. cit.,* Vol. XXX (1942), pp. 164 ff.
[5] *Op. cit.,* p. 67.
[6] *Kerygma und Mythos,* pp. 128–29.

interpretation of the Gospel, aiming at a language that will carry meaning today, plays its part in the formulation offered.

We still would urge, however, that an unnecessary depreciation of the "mythology" used in connection with the cross, the resurrection, the giving of the Spirit, etc., weakens any version of the Gospel. As we saw in connection with the message of Paul, the pictorial vehicles suggesting expiation and victory over demonic powers have perennial significance and need not be misleading to moderns. No doubt specific elements in the resurrection narratives as in the birth narratives of the Gospels can be a liability to the deepest Christian understanding. The oral tradition gathered up exotic elements and foreign bodies which then found a place in our written Gospels. But the church's early witness to the resurrection of Christ from the dead, that is, his exaltation as Lord and his entrance into glory, attended by signs and prodigies, carries insights which are lost in attempts at more sober statement. Yet Bultmann is right in holding that the meaning of Christ's resurrection can only be rightly grasped by the man who knows what it is to die with Christ on the cross.

We have dealt at some length with this scholar's proposal just because it offers us a concrete and masterly instance of the issues involved in dealing with the language of faith. But similar observations could have been made in connection with the modern liberal version of Christianity. Here too a modern philosophy offered the framework for the formulation, a philosophy similarly inclined to rid itself of obsolete myths and images. Where the liberal made an effort to keep in touch with the deeper intention of these symbols he provided an important contribution to the preaching of the Gospel in changing circumstances. Where he hastily rejected such symbols he

impoverished the faith. Hosts of men today are alienated from
the Christian faith in part because orthodoxy has misused the
language of faith. But many others remaining in the religious
institutions have failed to grasp the wholeness of their confession because the full force of the classic imagery has been
attenuated by modernism.

Today we have a new opportunity to interpret the Scripture in its fullness. Passing beyond orthodoxy and modernism
we find our lead in a postliberal recovery of the Bible and of
the early Christian message. This movement has restored to us
a fully positive grasp of the New Testament without any re-
linquishment of historical criticism. It has highlighted the good
news of the divine action as everywhere witnessed in these
writings. It has taught us, moreover, to find the perennial
"word of God" for men and for ourselves in the saving events
there reported, a word that speaks through the Scripture and
one, therefore, not distinct from the word witnessed by the
church through the centuries. It is in the act of faith that this
word is grasped, understood and appropriated.

Our final step, however, has been to warn against too abstract an understanding of this word and too purely religious
an interpretation of the message. God deals with man in his
wholeness and his revelation is the answer to all our most
human actualities, to the full compass of our manifold experience, and to all our creaturely questing and miscarriage. His
revelation is a grace shed upon the ancient and perennial
annals of the heart in all their shame and glory. If this be the
case, how then can the story of God with man be told without
giving full value to the incomparable legacies of the religious
imagination in the Scriptures, resting as they do upon symbols
and myths rooted deep in the historical life of man?

It is true that we must ultimately rest the appeal of the Gospel upon the work of God in men's hearts, or, as many would say, upon the divine word. But how can this word be dissociated from the earthen vessels, the human idiom and rhetoric, by one form or another of which it has always made contact with the actualities of human experience and the life of the heart? Of all human activities religion most involves the dramatic aspects of the life of the soul, including its ardors, revulsions, terrors and joys. These features of experience must be recognized in the language and rites of faith or men will not know that the Gospel really deals with what is important to them. As Brother George Every has said of a great deal of current pallid religious art: it has all the insipidity of the secular Christmas card, "but El Greco gives a sense of interior experience, of something that tore at the very vitals of man." [7] This is a strong way of stating the matter, but adequate Christian language must do this, and therefore the most potent, dramatic and paradoxical imagery is essential. This the preacher and theologian will find in Scripture, and in its interpretation he will find analogous language drawn from the life of today.

[7] *Christian Discrimination* (London: S.P.C.K., 1940), p. 59.

index

[Page numbers in italics indicate quotation or discussion]

index of scripture passages

OLD TESTAMENT

NEW TESTAMENT